On a hundred degree Monday, July 23, 2007, a pack of Hells Angels arranged their motorcycles into a pair of tight columns like old-fashioned horse cavalry and abandoned modern Reno for the stark wastelands of northern Nevada.

Those wastelands, and other arid and useless islands in the West, are what remains of historic America: The America that invented the telephone, the light bulb, the aeroplane and Mark Twain; a refuge for iconoclasts, libertarians, fringe believers, grifters, scoundrels, outlaws and saints, crank cooks and prophets, luddites and whores. There is elbow room in Northern Nevada. There is an absolute minimum number of police per square mile. There is widespread contempt for political correctness, for nanny laws written by ideologues and for the very many laws written by corporate lobbyists. Self-reliance, pragmatism, physical toughness and minding your own business are considered virtues. It is a version of America that is disappearing both geographically and psychologically as shadows disappear into a deepening twilight. And the mostly middle aged to aged men in that pack of Angels that day were that disappearing America's poster boys.

...the law worketh wrath: for where there is no law, there is no transgression.

Romans Chapter 4, Verse 15

Framing Dave Burgess:
A True Story About Hells Angels, Sex And Justice

Donald Charles Davis

Contents

The Hells Angel

On a hundred degree Monday, July 23, 2007, a pack of Hells Angels arranged their motorcycles into a pair of tight columns like old-fashioned horse cavalry and abandoned modern Reno for the stark wastelands of northern Nevada.

Those wastelands, and other arid and useless islands in the West, are what remains of historic America: The America that invented the telephone, the light bulb, the aeroplane and Mark Twain; a refuge for iconoclasts, libertarians, fringe believers, grifters, scoundrels, outlaws and saints, crank cooks and prophets, luddites and whores. There is elbow room in Northern Nevada. There is an absolute minimum number of police per square mile. There is widespread contempt for political correctness, for nanny laws written by ideologues and for the very many laws written by corporate lobbyists. Self-reliance, pragmatism, physical toughness and minding your own business are considered virtues. It is a version of America that is disappearing both geographically and psychologically as shadows disappear into a deepening twilight. And the mostly middle aged to aged men in that pack of Angels that day were that disappearing America's poster boys.

Their dominant foundation myth declares that the Hells Angels began in San Bernardino, California in 1948. An alternative version claims they were founded in Fontana in 1947. And they were named for an Army Air Squadron. The original club had chapters as far away as San Francisco by 1953 which was also around the time the club began to become notorious. They became the panic that results when young veterans with Post Traumatic Stress Disorder – on cheap Army surplus motorcycles in an economy built on virtually disposable laboring jobs – encounter rock n' roll and a passing social construct called juvenile delinquency.

Hunter Thompson wrote about them in a book published in 1966 and sub-titled *The Strange and Terrible Saga of the Outlaw Motorcycle Gangs*. About half of Thompson's book is a novel. But by simply writing about the Hells Angels Thompson became an icon. Thompson and the Angels, Thompson assured us, both had substance abuse problems. And now, investigative journalists assure us, the Hells Angels are one of the leading causes of substance abuse problems. They fight with other "outlaw gangs," we read over and over, for control of the "drug trade" and control of "drug routes" and "drug territories."

Since before Thompson, the idea of the Hells Angels has always been bigger than their reality. First they were famous rapists. Then they were the saviors of the hippies' inalienable right to drugs – when Bay Area Angels chased the predatory drug dealers out of the Haight. The club still has a little patch that says, "You can trust me. I'm a Hells Angel." They were good hippies and Merry Pranksters. Then, after Altamont, they became evil hippies like the Manson family. Sonny Barger, the most famous Hells Angel of all, has called the seventies "our gangster years." Federal police began calling the Angels an organized crime syndicate in the 1980s. That might be the most ridiculous thing said about the Angels yet. Many of them are criminals as a matter of principle but they are about as organized as a herd of cats.

And now that their time has almost passed, the world has begun to wax nostalgic for the Hells Angels and for all the motorcycle outlaws. Outlaws live that meeker men may live through them. Since Vietnam, outlaw motorcycle clubs have become one of America's most successful exports. There are now outlaw clubs on every continent except Antarctica and "Hells Angels" has become a metonym for all outlaw bikers. The actual Hells Angels are a confederation of at least 429 local clubs, or charters, in 49 countries. There are probably about 6,500 Hells Angels in all but their hold on the popular imagination, particularly in the English speaking world, is much greater than their numbers would suggest. Multiple television documentaries and many "true crime" genre books about motorcycle outlaws appear year after year. The Angels are almost always portrayed as professional criminals.

The popular cable melodrama *Sons of Anarchy* is unabashedly based on the Hells Angels. The show romanticizes its fictional outlaws as a kind of Mafia crime family. Kurt Sutter, who produces *Sons of Anarchy*, has described his show as an "homage." He has also attributed the success of his program to "vicarious badassary," which is probably about right. Sonny Barger likes the show. He has appeared on it. Sutter seems to be inspired by Barger as Tom Mix was inspired by Wyatt Earp.

Kerrie Droban, who has published three books about outlaw bikers, has said her intention in the first of those was to give her readers the "vicarious experience of being a Hells Angel." Another biker book author, the ATF undercover agent Jay Dobyns, has described his time trying to infiltrate the Hells Angels in Arizona as the "ultimate bad boy fantasy." William Queen, who infiltrated the Mongols Motorcycle Club using the name Billy St. John, wrote more astutely: "I watched the Mongols hugging and high-fiving, laughing and toasting the new year with beer. They exchanged war stories and put their tattooed arms tightly around one another. They put their arms around me. They freely and sincerely expressed their love for one another and for me. It was sincere. I knew that they honestly loved Billy St. John. And at that moment I desperately wanted to be Billy St. John."

And still, despite all the attention they currently receive, motorcycle outlaws are actually much more interesting than they are usually made out to be. They cannot be truthfully stuffed into a box with the label "True Crime" on the side. They illuminate America more than all that has and will be written and televised on the subject of motorcycle outlaws will ever illuminate them. Except for the occasional dissertation, they are never regarded through an historical, sociological or anthropological lens.

There is virtually no thoughtful journalism produced about outlaws in part because Thompson famously portrayed himself as a victim of the Angels' brutish violence. He left the impression that it is actually dangerous to be in their presence and to ask them questions. Or at least, Thompson left that impression fifty years ago. After Thompson's brilliant hatchet job, motorcycle outlaws became shy around reporters they don't know or trust. So after Thompson, most clubs enacted formal rules that forbid members from speaking to the press.

And most significantly, reporters have an easy alternative source for learning about the motorcycle outlaw counterculture – which is the police. All reporters are expected to do in return is write exactly what their police sources want them to write.

Police, particularly federal police, are tasked with waging war on groups like the Hells Angels so it is in their self-interest to vilify their prey. Most reporters don't question what they are told by cops. Most editors and publishers consider cops to be bullet proof sources. And, modern police have become practiced at cynically manipulating mass media to serve police ends. Learning to manipulate mass media, particularly television, is now one of the acknowledged attributes of "professional policing."

Consequently, almost everything most people think about the Hells Angels and their world, the world of outlaw motorcycle clubs, is wrong – which seems to suit most people just fine. Kerrie Droban, or her literary agent, is correct. Most Americans now do live the most interesting parts of their lives vicariously. They know their world, they experience war and sport, they comprehend their economy and their government mostly from new media like cable television and the billion blossoms of the internet. In the last decade, young Americans have begun to know life through video games, which are computer simulations of life. Increasingly, citizens in all the first world nations have become like the doomed mob in Plato's Allegory of the Cave: People in chains, condemned to face a blank wall and informed by flickering shadows of reality. Most of what people think about the Hells Angels is what they wish were true. So what is actually most interesting about the Hells Angels Motorcycle Club is the influence it exerts on the imaginations of citizens in the developed world, particularly in the imaginations of men. The mere idea of the Hells Angels plucks a primal chord in men's souls.

There are obvious reasons why men whose alleged behavior is almost universally regarded as wrong inspire admiration. Mainly, the Hells Angels Motorcycle Club is a conservative institution that continues to epitomize post World War II ideals about who and what a man should be. And a certain percentage of First World men still embrace those traditional ideals.

Post-Vietnam America has rushed headlong into a repudiation of the first 200 years of American History. "Not God bless America! Goddamn America," as the Reverend

4

Jeremiah Wright put it. Simultaneously, the sorts of jobs men used to have and that helped define men's identities, unionized and well paying jobs in manufacturing and heavy industry, were replaced by "service economy" and "knowledge worker" jobs that women could do just as well. Social and commercial forces forced women to work full time. Women no longer "make homes." Women now compete with men for an essentially shrinking pool of increasingly marginal jobs because most families simply cannot survive on one paycheck. Exclusively male institutions have been widely outlawed as part of the same social transformation. And, although most men are now compelled to attend extra years in school and go into debt to pay for that "education," few of them now know how to actually make or repair tangible, useful things. Most men now work at ambiguous jobs in offices. Post millennial men do not sell their labor as much as they sell their acquiescence. Job security, and so life itself, now depends on skills like building consensus and avoiding conflict.

A mere 60 years ago, when the rules that govern the motorcycle outlaw counterculture were developed, that counterculture's rules reflected the mores of American society at large. And, much of what seemed normal and ordinary then is seen as actually pathological now. So it is becoming increasingly easier to portray motorcycle outlaws as pathological. Most outlaws are men who don't fit well into society at large. They fit well in groups like the Hells Angels. And, they are the same sort of men who tend to do well at war.

*****

All the world's motorcycle clubs are products of the Great Depression, the Second World War and Vietnam. The Hells Angels were formed by veterans after World War II, were greatly reinforced by Vietnam Vets and continue to be renewed by veterans of American wars in the Middle East. Policemen and writers who front for policemen usually portray outlaw bikers as, if not crime syndicates, at least as mutual protection societies comprised of career criminals. In fact, clubs like the Hells Angels think of themselves as elite brotherhoods analogous to small combat units. For most outlaws criminality is beside the point. Criminality is simply preferable to working at McDonalds.

5

While not writing about motorcycle clubs at all but instead about other groups of men, a couple of contemporary writers named Sebastian Junger and his friend, the late Tim Hetherington, defined the essence of groups like the Hells Angels. Speaking in an independent film called *Which Way Is the Front Line From Here*, Junger said Hetherington was intrigued by "the truth about combat as a form of bonding.... Tim called it the Man Eden." Junger and Hetherington were first moved to articulate their ideas about men who fight beside one another when they collaborated on the Oscar nominated film *Restrepo*.

James Brabazon, another collaborator on that film thinks, "War is the only opportunity that men have in society to love each other unconditionally and it's understanding the depth of emotion of men at war that Tim was fascinated with."

To which Junger adds "The experience of being part of a group like that," the Man Eden of a forward operating base, "is not reproducible in society."

Because there are so few motorcycle outlaws and because of the limits of his own experience, Junger is blind to the fact that that is exactly what outlaw motorcycle clubs are – socially isolated examples of Man Eden. That is why so many outlaws are combat veterans. The feeling of belonging to a band of brothers is part of the Hells Angels appeal to men who have never been in combat or ridden with a motorcycle club. The Man Eden that intrigued Hetherington intrigues almost all men and it seems so basic to masculinity that it can be described in numerous ways: Obviously, for example, as a vestige of the American frontier experience, or as a folkway that probably predates *Beowulf* or as an analogue to the ancient and universal "small hunting group."

The most cogent proclamation of the attitudes and values of outlaw motorcycle clubs and their wide masculine appeal is found in William James' often mentioned but practically forgotten essay "The Moral Equivalent of War."

In the lead to his obituary in 1910, the New York *Times* called James "America's foremost philosophical writer" and the "virtual founder of the modern school of psychology." James' students included Theodore Roosevelt, George Santayana, W. E. B. Du Bois, G. Stanley Hall, Gertrude Stein and Walter Lippmann. He formed the ideas in his essay for a speech at Stanford in 1906, the same year his former student Roosevelt was awarded the Nobel Prize for negotiating an end to the appallingly violent Russo-Japanese War. Because it is now so rarely read, and because his words can now seem so antique, it is probably appropriate to review at least some of what James said a little more than a century ago.

With a view towards the tragedy that had just occurred in Korea and Manchuria James began by saying something that once made sense to most of the literate world:

"There is something highly paradoxical in the modern man's relation to war," James said. "Ask all our millions, north and south, whether they would vote now (were such a thing possible) to have our war for the Union expunged from history, and the record of a peaceful transition to the present time substituted for that of its marches and battles, and probably hardly a handful of eccentrics would say yes. Those ancestors, those efforts, those memories and legends, are the most ideal part of what we now own together, a sacred spiritual possession worth more than all the blood poured out. Yet ask those same people whether they would be willing, in cold blood, to start another civil war now to gain another similar possession, and not one man or woman would vote for the proposition."

The father of American psychology, went on to say: "The earlier men were hunting men, and to hunt a neighboring tribe, kill the males, loot the village and possess the females, was the most profitable, as well as the most exciting, way of living."

"Modern war is so expensive that we feel trade to be a better avenue to plunder; but modern man inherits all the innate pugnacity and all the love of glory of his ancestors. Showing war's irrationality and horror is of no effect on him. The horrors make the fascination. War is the strong life; it is life in extremis…."

"History is a bath of blood."

"Patriotism no one thinks discreditable; nor does any one deny that war is the romance of history. But inordinate ambitions are the soul of any patriotism, and the possibility of violent death the soul of all romance."

"The militarily-patriotic and the romantic-minded everywhere, and especially the professional military class, refuse to admit for a moment that war may be a transitory phenomenon in social evolution. The notion of a sheep's paradise like that revolts, they say, our higher imagination. Where then would be the steeps of life? If war had ever

7

stopped, we should have to re-invent it, on this view, to redeem life from flat degeneration."

"No scorn, no hardness, no valor any more! Fie upon such a cattleyard of a planet!"

"…weaklings and mollycoddles may not end by making everything else disappear from the face of nature."

"Martial virtues must be the enduring cement; intrepidity, contempt of softness, surrender of private interest, obedience to command, must still remain the rock upon which states are built."

James was a pacifist, and during his lifetime his ideas were never considered insane, but he would certainly be silenced by criticism today. His proclamations about the dark heart of man seem anachronistic – as if the essential nature of man is shaped by modern forces of social control rather than evolution. Were he to give his speech at Stanford today, James would certainly be booed.

A couple of impeccable liberals may help make the point.

In an intelligent and reasonable column in 2013, David Brooks, the less likely to be booed New York *Times* political and cultural commentator, described Ethan Edwards, the character portrayed by John Wayne in John Ford's once classic film *The Searchers*, as a man "caught on the wrong side of a historical transition." Brooks sees Wayne's Edwards as racist, sexist and homicidal. He was, Brooks allows, the sort of "classic western hero" who tamed the West and in so doing made himself "obsolete."

"Once the western towns have been pacified," Brooks wrote, "there's no need for his capacity for violence, nor his righteous fury." At least not until the next time the nation needs to win a war. The columnist is really talking about the current marginalization of the kind of men who fought all the wars America "never lost," conquered the wilderness and made the industrial revolution possible.

Brooks also notices that 96 percent of American men between 25 and 54 years old worked in 1954 but today only 80 percent of the same demographic are employed. "Part of the situation," Brooks continues, "is that many men simply do not want to put themselves in positions they find humiliating. A high school student doesn't want to persist in a school where he feels looked down on. A guy in his 50s doesn't want to find

8

work in a place where he'll be told what to do by savvy young things."

And so Brooks describes the attraction of the idea of the Hells Angels. Hells Angels do not permit themselves to be humiliated. They are men who hate being looked down on. They live in an alternative world where honor rarely coincides with acquiescence. Hells Angels will fight to the death over an insult. They are the men other men wish they were when those other men are made to feel weak and powerless and out of control. The character Ethan Edwards could have been a Hells Angel. Before their were Hells Angels, men like them wrested Texas from the Comanche Empire.

Other influential commentators seem less sympathetic to the existential plight of contemporary men than Brooks. For example, the seemingly omnipresent Michael Kimmel, whose hustle it is to be "among the leading researchers and writers on men and masculinity in the world today."

Kimmel, whose side job is being a professor at the State University of New York at Stony Brook – and where better to study masculinity – has written frequently and influentially about what he calls the "contemporary crisis of masculinity" which is "a general confusion and malaise about the meaning of manhood." Kimmel would see almost everything James believed about men to be historical and psychological delusions. While many contemporary artists look at the world and see a looming dystopia, Kimmel sees the perfecting of humanity. In *The Shriver Report*, published in 2009, Kimmel wrote:

"Declaring America to be a woman's nation, while deliberately provocative, does not mean we are, but just as surely it does mean we no longer live in a man's world, underscoring a significant trend of the gradual, undeniable, and irreversible progress toward gender equality in every arena of American life – from the public sector (economic life, politics, the military) to private life (work-family balance, marital contracts, sexuality). Women have successfully entered every arena of public life, and today many women are as comfortable in the corporate boardroom, the athletic playing field, the legal and medical professions, and the theater of military operations as previous generations of women might have been in the kitchen."

"And they've done it amazingly fast. It is within the last half-century that the workplace has been so dramatically

9

transformed, that the working world depicted in the hit TV show *Mad Men* (about Madison Avenue advertising executives in the early 1960s) looks so anachronistic as to be nearly unrecognizable. For both women and men, these dramatic changes have come at such a dizzying pace that many Americans are searching for the firmer footing of what they imagine was a simpler time, a bygone era in which everyone knew his or her place."

Kimmel goes on to describe the sorts of things William James and Theodore Roosevelt considered self-evident truths as "masculine myths."

"For significant numbers of younger men," Kimmel continues, "remote corners of cyberspace are the newest incarnation of the *Little Rascals'* 'He-Man Woman Haters Club,' the tree house with the sign that says 'No Gurls Allowed.' These types of masculinists tend to rely on archaic notions of the essential, natural, and binary masculine and feminine."

Kimmel's borrowed turn of phrase about woman haters was also uttered by Jane Sims, a reporter for the London, Ontario *Free Press* while she was covering an infamous motorcycle outlaw mass murder case. After seeing the defendants at trial Sims told Toronto *Star* reporter Peter Edwards that the accused men "sounded like the He-Man Woman Haters Club from the old Little Rascals television series." So the Hells Angels are probably the sort of "archaic" masculinists Kimmel thinks the world should reject.

But, it is impossible, after reading dead white men like James and Roosevelt and then reading contemporary opinion makers like Kimmel, not to think that one side or the other must be very wrong. Modern social orthodoxy, or "political correctness," seems symptomatic of a nation and a culture at war with its own history. After Vietnam, after the civil rights movement, the women's movement, gay liberation and the commencement of Nixon's war on drugs, an elite ruling class emerged that appears to think that human nature can best be perfected utilizing the power of the state. Cops call this new relationship between America and Americans "pro-active policing" and in the second decade of the new millennium it is evident in Michael Bloomberg's New York. Bloomberg believes, for example, that society is better when police can simply detain anyone they want and search them in violation of the Fourth Amendment prohibition on unreasonable searches. When a federal judge named Shira Scheindlin told Bloomberg's police to stop it, Bloomberg held a press conference at which he announced, "This is a very dangerous decision made by a judge who I don't think understands how policing works." And Bloomberg may have been right because a blatant disregard for the Constitution and basic human rights is how modern policing "works."

Nationally, the same politicians who funded and promulgated the recent, interminable wars in the Middle East – and so have swelled the ranks of motorcycle outlaws – think nothing of condemning the timeless actions of the men who have had to fight those wars.

Like, in September 2012 United States Marines were widely described as "inhuman" for urinating on the bodies of dead Taliban. All combat veterans, and virtually every man who has lived in the last 200,000 years, would have found the conduct of those Marines to be at least understandable. Some percentage of those men would find pissing on the bodies of their enemies laugh out loud hilarious.

But Debbie Wasserman Schultz, at the time the Chairwoman of the Democratic National Committee and a rising political star, speaking on Bill Maher's television show on *HBO*, condemned the men fighting her war for not fighting it correctly. The same week a Marine Staff Sergeant was being court-martialed for "desecration of human remains," "posing for unofficial photographs with human casualties," "failing to properly supervise junior Marines" and not reporting misconduct, Shultz, speaking very carefully as if her most heartfelt wish was to build consensus and avoid conflict, said "Let's remember that this is the United States of America. The greatest country in the world that is the country that we hold ourselves up as a shining example. That conduct, and I represent a lot of wonderful 18 year old kids in the Twenty-Third District in South Florida, and I wouldn't expect that conduct out of any of them no matter what their level of maturity is and it's unacceptable in any way shape or form." The entire population of the television studio, which might not have contained a single combat veteran, enthusiastically cheered.

*****

It is hard to imagine that Schultz and Kimmel and others who share their reality would see anything but

11

criminality in the month Northern California Angels had at the end of September and the beginning of October 2011. Two Angels were murdered that month in a concatenation of tragedies that both William James and William Shakespeare, but not Debbie Wasserman Schultz or Michael Kimmel, would have found to be innately, imperfectably human.

On September 23rd that year, a small group of Hells Angels and members of the Vagos Motorcycle Club shared a hotel in Sparks, Nevada named John Ascuaga's Nugget Casino Resort. Both groups were there for an annual motorcycle rally centered in nearby Reno called "Street Vibrations." The Nugget was the Vagos' official hotel and more than 200 of them were staying there. The dozen or so Angels, who were all from San Jose, had a souvenir and tee shirt stand set up outside the Nugget.

And, that night the 51 year old president of the Angels' San Jose charter, Jeffrey "Jethro" Pettigrew – who worked not as a drug dealer or professional criminal but as a heavy equipment operator for the city of San Jose – took some time in the big hours of the evening to roam about the casino floor and say hello and shake hands with every Vago he met. Pettigrew, who was one of the most esteemed and influential Hells Angels in the West, was paying his respects to the members of the other club. The maxim in the outlaw world is "Give respect, get respect." Frequently, Pettigrew would lay his big hand on a Vagos shoulder or gently pat the other man on the back. Because the outlaw world is frequently self-dramatizing, some Vagos feared that the big cooler a couple of Angels prospects, or apprentices, hauled around behind Pettigrew might hold guns. But it was only full of beer.

There had been several violent confrontations between Angels and Vagos in the previous 16 months – with the most violent being a gunfight between Angels and Vagos in Chino Valley, Arizona near Prescott, in August 2010. There the middle class homes that served as the informal clubhouses of the Vagos and Angels were only a block apart. The Vagos scheduled a birthday party on the same day the Angels were having a barbecue and those two local chapters did not get along well with each other. The Angels, who had been drinking, saw a small pack of Vagos travelling to the party down the street as a threat. And, in the space of a minute, fifty shots were fired and five men were wounded. There was also a fistfight in Kingman, Arizona; a murder in Bakersfield,

California, and another brawl outside a Starbucks in Santa Cruz where the local Vagos and Hells Angels did not like each other. That brawl led professional journalists at the *Huffington Post* and *Fox News* to report that the members of the two clubs were "fighting over Starbucks."

But, Pettigrew's San Jose charter got along well with their local Vagos. Some members of the two clubs In San Jose had played little league baseball together and had known each other all their lives. So Pettigrew was trying to encourage peace. All the Vagos leadership was staying in that hotel and they all also wanted to keep the peace. But one Vago, the vice-president of the Los Angeles chapter of the Vagos, a mean drunk named Stuart Gary "Jabbers" Rudnick, was determined to start a fight. He knew his club had the Angels outnumbered, and according to some Vagos who were there Rudnick hoped to collect a Hells Angels patch as a war trophy. So when Pettigrew touched Jabbers Rudnick's back Jabbers began to complain loudly that Pettigrew had touched the patch he wore on his back, which is a breech of outlaw etiquette.

Jabbers Rudnick then proceeded to taunt and hector Pettigrew off and on over the next hour. Senior Vagos intervened at least twice. They thanked Pettigrew for his patience, agreed that they were all "too old for this shit" and told Rudnick to stop or leave the casino floor. Rudnick did neither and finally Pettigrew had had enough. By the code of honor to which both clubs subscribed, Pettigrew could not allow himself to be disrespected because to do so would be to allow his patch, as a symbol of all Hells Angels everywhere, to be disrespected. "So are we done here or what," Rudnick taunted the last time Pettigrew turned to walk away. "Are we going to shake hands?"

Pettigrew marched back up to Rudnick, declared, "I don't shake hands with bitches," and hit Rudnick in the head with a bottle. Rudnick fell and quickly crawled away to safety behind some slot machines. But as he crawled a small corner of the casino exploded with violence. In the honor driven world of outlaw clubs, when one member fights all members must fight. Pettigrew was beset by Vagos. He pulled a gun.

Pettigrew, who wore a prosthetic leg as the result of a motorcycle accident, kicked, punched and pistol whipped every Vago he could reach. In return Vagos stabbed Pettigrew multiple times including one wound that almost cut off his nose.

13

The San Jose Hells Angels sergeant at arms, a man named Cesar Villagrana, stood side by side with Pettigrew. Villagrana pulled a gun and began firing above the crowd saying "Get down! Get down!" Two Vagos named Leonard Ramirez and Diego Garcia were shot although it is still unclear which of the two Angels shot them.

One of the Vagos both Villagrana and Pettigrew kicked was Robert "Corporate Bob" Wiggins, the vice-president of the Orange County, California Vagos. He heard Pettigrew's last words which were, "This is what happens when you fuck with the Hells Angels."

A San Jose Vago and a 54-year-old grandfather named Ernesto Manuel "Romeo" Gonzalez returned from dinner at a nearby burger joint just in time for the melee. "When the fight ensued, I backed up," Gonzalez said, weeping, at his eventual trial. "I didn't want any part of it…. I thought it was done. As I approached inside the disco, I still see them walking. At the same time and same moment, I have a brother (Vago) on the ground. Then they start approaching him and kicking." Gonzalez produced a semi-automatic handgun and fatally shot Pettigrew five times in the back. He would later say that it was his duty to protect his club brother Corporate Bob and that he also intended to kill Villagrana but missed. The shooting was over in less than a minute – about the time it took Villagrana to empty two magazines.

That weekend, Brook Baldwin reported on *CNN* that Pettigrew's murder was the result of "a turf war! And, it all started when the Vagos tried to muscle in on a Hells Angels hangout. That being a Starbucks in downtown Santa Cruz in California."

Gonzalez spent the night of the shooting in a different hotel and went on the run the next day. His greatest fear was retribution by the Angels, not the law. He was apprehended in San Francisco seven days later by a campus cop near the University of California at San Francisco campus. After he was arrested he asked the cop to hurry him to jail because he feared the Hells Angels might find him at any moment.

As part of a negotiated plea deal, Villagrana eventually confessed to one count of battery with a deadly weapon and a single count of challenge to fight with a deadly weapon.

Rudnick was expelled from the Vagos two days after he started the fight. He soon agreed to inform on his former club. He pled guilty to conspiracy to commit second degree murder and was set free. As part of his plea deal he testified against Gonzalez who was found guilty of first degree murder and five other charges.

Pettigrew's funeral was October 15th at the Oak Hill Funeral Home and Memorial Park in San Jose. The cemetery was surrounded by police and there was widespread media speculation that the Vagos might show up to start trouble. Four thousand mourners including Cesar Villagrana, Sonny Barger and numerous Hells Angel charter presidents attended. One of the mourners was the 52 year old Sergeant at Arms for the Santa Cruz charter and a former member of the San Jose charter named Steve "187" Tausan. Tausan brought his nine year old son to the funeral with him.

About midway through the service, as Pettigrew's casket was being loaded into a hearse for the drive to the grave, Tausan got into a heated argument with another Hells Angel named Steve Ruiz in the driveway just outside the chapel. The argument was over the actions of other Angels as Pettigrew fought and died. Had everyone done everything they could to save Pettigrew? Had any Hells Angel acted like a coward? The dispute quickly became a one sided fist fight. Tausan, a former middleweight boxer, was significantly larger than Ruiz and he quickly knocked the other man on his back.

Ruiz pulled a handgun from inside his vest and fired two shots about three seconds apart. Tausan was mortally wounded. A dozen Angels subdued and disarmed the killer, stripped him of his colors, put a baseball cap on his head and shoved him into a car. As the funeral proceeded Tausan was carried to the police line. There was no ambulance and the police were in no hurry to call one. One policeman advised his fellow officers to "Let him bleed out." Tausan waited fifteen minutes for treatment and died at a San Jose hospital about fifteen minutes after that.

Hells Angels washed down the shooting scene. Police assumed Ruiz, whose name they did not yet know, was dead. Every Hells Angel at the funeral was detained for hours and questioned. That night police exhumed Pettigrew's remains to search his coffin for Ruiz' body or other clues. The coffin only held Pettigrew.

The occasionally farcical search for Ruiz, or his body, lasted four months. The investigation included a Swat raid on the Stockton home of a woman whose daughter had once gone on a date with Ruiz. Ruiz was finally captured by police an hour after checking into a Days Inn in Fremont at the end of February.

The murders of Pettigrew and Tausan were so melodramatic that reporters practically gloated over the tragedies for months. Television executives, prosecutors and cops all cynically exploit the public's fascination with violent events like these. But what the murders most represented was the depth of the commitment men must make when they join an outlaw motorcycle club.

Joining the Hells Angels is much more serious than getting married. It is even more serious than getting your new bride's name tattooed on your arm.

Outlaws, regardless of their ethnicity, live by a Viking code. An outlaw must be ever ready to embrace his defining moment, whether it is crawling behind a bank of slot machines like Jabbers Rudnick; murdering a club brother, in the midst of an argument over honor, like Steve Ruiz; or going down fighting like Jethro Pettigrew. Most men spend some time in their lives imagining what they will do in the defining moments of their lives but not many of them are willing to do more than daydream.

This necessary fatalism is one of many reasons why so few men are cut out to become Hells Angels.

*****

In addition to a willingness and ability to fight at the drop of a hat, another rare, if obvious, qualification for becoming a Hells Angel is an affection for riding a motorcycle tens of thousands of miles a year in all kinds of weather.

The Hells Angels traversing northern Nevada on July 23, 2007 were beginning a motorcycle ride that would cover at least five thousand miles. The pack included men from Reno and Oakland and several points in between. Aside from being icons of the way many American men like to think of themselves, these Angels were tourists on an adventure. The motorcycles were followed by a caravan of cars transporting wives, children and girlfriends. They were all bound for the Hells Angels annual national run which was being held that year in a picturesque Ozarks town named Eureka Springs. But, their destination mattered less to them than the motorcycle ride they shared and their shared illusion of escape.

16

Before they left Reno they were already on Interstate 80 – the Lincoln Highway, a road that has traversed America for a century and is one of the three great highways that cross the nation from sea to shining sea. On a map the road seems to wind like a rattlesnake but that is only an illusion caused by the great distances maps portray. Up close the road is mostly straight, lightly travelled and it sings to those who follow it. The wind whispered in the men's ears. They could hear the singing and whispering over their engines' booms and roars.

The highway parallels the remnants of the transcontinental railroad which accelerated the transformation of America from what it once was and what hollow men on television still proclaim it to be into something radically different. The Hells Angels stuck mostly to the left lane, passing the slower traffic headed for Winnemucca, Elko and eventually Salt Lake. The heavens were flawless. The great sage desert was God's Zen garden. At fleeting and unexpected moments little knots of the last mustangs spied on the concrete ribbon before retreating back into the modern west – the impoverished west, the atomic west, the west of strip malls, ghost towns and history. In the wide open spaces it is still easy to believe that the historic America is something real.

Hour after hour the desert sun reddened the men's tanned faces. They were blessed by the wind at their backs so their hearts were light despite the baggage they carried from their sometimes tragic, sometimes cinematic, authority defying lives. And of course they also carried with them all the baggage that comes with becoming a Hells Angel.

The pack passed almost everyone they met on the road. They would emerge out of the heat waves on the western horizon like a mirage, grow into something real and anachronistic then disappear into the long shadows. The people they passed remembered them. For most of those reminiscers a glimpse of these outlaws was something memorable that happened to them – something splendid to tell their grandchildren someday.

Miles behind the motorcycles and the caravan of cars, two more Hells Angels travelled the same road in a remarkably unromantic 1999, air conditioned, white Freightliner motor home. The Freightliner was the "chase truck" for the pack. It carried tools, much of the baggage for the men in the pack and along with the baggage it held the pack's drug stash. It was towing two motorcycles in a trailer. If a motorcycle in the pack broke down, the chase truck would stop and trade the broken down bike for one of the ones in the trailer. The two Hells Angels in the Freightliner were David William Burgess, the owner of the Freightliner and just four days short of his 55th birthday, and 37 year old Shayne Deloy Waldron.

Dave Burgess is an interesting man. He was very prosperous. Like many Hells Angels he was artistically inclined. Some Angels are gun enthusiasts, mixed martial artists, stock brokers, thieves, smugglers, actors and pimps. A disproportionate percentage of them have a creative side and many of them express that by building custom motorcycles or sketching tattoos. Some of them make music, take photographs, write and paint. Most of them are interesting men. Sonny Barger now likes to write novels. Rusty Coones, the president of the San Fernando Valley charter, is a bike builder, an actor and he plays in an internationally known heavy metal band named Attika 7. Dave Burgess liked to write, garden and take photographs. He operated a website that was well known in motorcycle circles. He was always surrounded by beautiful women. He liked to call himself the "Alpha Male." He had an interesting past, a promising future and he had always wanted to be a Hells Angel.

Dave Burgess' role models were examples of traditional masculinity. His father, Big Jim Burgess was a lifer Marine who had served in the Second World War, Korea, and Vietnam. His brother Sherm had also served in Vietnam and his cousin Steve was a disabled Vietnam veteran. He grew up around the Marine Corps. His mother worked at the Marine Corps Recruit Depot in San Diego. Burgess says he "was pretty much raised there."

Burgess met his first Hells Angel when he was fifteen, at a love-in at La Jolla Cove in early 1968. "Big Brother and the Holding Company was playing a free concert that day." Burgess remembers. "That was the first time I ever saw a Hells Angel and the beginning of my dream to become a member." The Angel was a newly patched member of the San Diego charter named Lurch. He later transferred to the Oakland charter and he and Burgess remained life-long friends. When Lurch died in 2012 Burgess wrote, "Do not feel too bad for Lurch. Lurch was a Hells Angel for more than 40 years and he was involved in more wild and fun times like that than ten people can experience in one lifetime."

The young Burgess met a custom bike builder named Porky who belonged to a motorcycle club called the Mescaleros. Porky lent Burgess a custom Harley, "a 1956, jockey shift Panhead with a raked frame and a 4 inch extended Springer front-end, no front fender and drag bars. And that's not all, it also had a fresh new black paint job and a flamed peanut tank and a flamed rear fender. He just said, take it for a putt, it's yours to use anytime you want." Burgess spent most of the summer he turned 18 riding that motorcycle.

He met more Hells Angels after he moved to Reno and he continued to ride motorcycles but he didn't actually begin the process of joining the Angels until he was almost forty. That's not unusual. The Angels want men who are both stable and brave. Burgess' experiences becoming an Angel were also typical.

He moved to Oakland for a year and began to hang around with his old friend Lurch. One of the Oakland Angels Burgess met was Elliot "Cisco" Valderrama. "Cisco has this very confidant air about himself and everyone is drawn to him," Burgess wrote years later. "I am not sure how to explain it, but Cisco treats everyone that he likes like they are his children. When you are with Cisco, you feel safe, and if he likes you, you are safe."

Burgess describes becoming a Hells Angel like this.

"One of the first things I noticed about Cisco and many other Hells Angels I have met all around the world is they not only have their club brothers to count on, but a lot of them seem to also have an entire network of family and close friends that are always near. When I started unofficially hanging around the club in Oakland and started meeting more Hells Angels, I noticed a lot of them had their own network of close friends that they treated like their own children. I would always think of my own little mob of family and close friends back in Reno and I was starting to see that the Hells Angels I was meeting not only treated the road the same way I did – we own the road when we are on our motorcycles – but they also treated their family and friends the same way I did. Before that time I never seriously thought of being in any kind of club, but I was beginning to see that I was like minded with many of these guys I was meeting."

"After about a year and getting to know a lot of the Members in Oakland, I was visiting with Cisco one evening and I told him I wanted to join his club. He said, 'Look David,

I am your friend, you can come around the club and clubhouse anytime you want. You can come to our parties and even come on our runs, but if you officially want to hang around the club and for some reason you do not make it, when you get rat-packed (which means to be beaten out by multiple assailants) I will have to kick you too.' And then he said, 'And besides, you already have money and more girls than you know what to do with. So why do you want to join my club?'"

"I told him, 'Yes, I do have all those things. But what I am looking for is brotherhood. When I am with Hells Angels, I feel like I am at home.' He just smiled and we went on to something else."

"Just as he was leaving that evening, he turned to me and said, 'I just want you to know something. If it doesn't work out for you, when we are rat-packing you I won't kick you as hard as everyone else will.' And then he turned and left. I am sure that over the many years I have known Cisco, there is more than one occasion that he may have wanted to kick me. And I am also sure that if I would have given him the chance, he would not have gone easy on me."

"One Friday night, I was hanging around out in front of the Oakland clubhouse while they were having church (the weekly club meeting) and after church the pack took off to the local watering hole down off of San Leandro Blvd. By this time I had gotten to know many of the members. One of the members I took to very quickly was 'SpiderMan.' SpiderMan came up to me and asked me if I was sure that I wanted to join his club. He told me that I may end up in prison for a very long time for crimes I do not commit. I may lose everything I have. The government hates Hells Angels and they will stop at nothing to put all of them behind bars. I asked him if the government could take away my brotherhood with the club. He said if I always continue to stand up for myself and for the club and I do the right thing, the club would never turn its back on me. That was good enough for me. Cisco and a few other members told me it was not going to be easy for me to get into the club because I had money and no one wanted it to look like someone could buy their way in. I told them all the same thing. I was going to become a member of the Hells Angels or die trying, and the rest is history."

"I can tell you this much, it was not easy getting in. But it was and still is more than worth it. I had my share of black eyes, cut lips, bloody noses, and stitches, but I also want

20

to tell you something; that's what makes it so much fun. We all know that we all went through it and we all survived. So now when we are together and things get rough, we all know that we can depend on each other in a tight spot. No true Hells Angel will ever run away from trouble but you can bet your ass he will run toward it if a club Brother is in a fix."

"Not all of being a Hells Angel is about fighting and getting into trouble, even though trouble has a way of following us around. Most of the best times I have had in my life are when I was with other Hells Angels. I got to live a life that most can only dream about. I was in Berdoo when the Hells Angels Motorcycle Club turned 50 years old. I was in Frisco when that Charter turned forty. I was in Oakland when it turned forty, and I was in New York City when they celebrated their thirtieth Anniversary. I was in Richmond, Ventura, Dago, Sonoma County, Merced County, Vallejo, Daly City, Shasta County, California Nomads, San Jose, Anchorage, Fairbanks, Spokane, Monterrey, Omaha, Charleston, Chicago, Lynn, Cleveland, Rochester, Raleigh, Berkshire County, Phoenix, and in Mesa for all their big parties. I was in Cave Creek, Tucson, Vegas, Fresno County, and Denver when they got their patches. I shared fine wine in my dining room with Hells Angel Brothers from New York City, Denmark, Norway, Vaduz, Berlin, Italy, Greece, Australia, New Zealand, Portugal, Canada, South America, and South Africa. I've traveled across the world and partied with club brothers at their clubhouses in England, Spain, France, Germany, Switzerland, Austria, Lichtenstein, and in Helsinki Finland. I have seen the world as only a select few men have ever seen it. I have shared many good times and have had the privilege to hang out and get to know many famous Hells Angels from all over the world. And I have also had the honor to be there and bury many good Hells Angels. I have done a lot and I have seen a lot and I would not trade those memories."

*****

That day driving through the wide open spaces was the last best day of Dave Burgess' life.

Burgess had never been convicted of a crime but federal authorities thought he was dangerous anyway because he was a Hells Angel. He and members of his extended family had been at odds with the law for most of his life. He had

21

enemies in several levels of government. That last best day, Burgess was in the middle of on ongoing battle with the Internal Revenue Service. But mostly Burgess was dangerous because of his prosperity and generosity.

The practice of federal justice is perverse and immoral. Something like ninety-three percent of all federal defendants plead guilty, not because they are actually guilty but because federal defendants are routinely overcharged so that federal prosecutors and investigators can gain "leverage" over them. The plea bargaining system mocks justice. Federal public defenders almost always insist that their clients agree to a plea bargain. Defendants who have money to pay for there own lawyers usually fair much better in federal court than defendants who must rely on public defenders. The situation is worst in big jurisdictions. Despite their reputation as Mafiosi, few Hells Angels can afford to pay their own lawyer. Dave Burgess' wealth gave him the power to change that. Anytime he wanted, in any case he wanted, Dave Burgess could level the playing field.

And Burgess tended to be larger than life and difficult to ignore. Burgess tells a tale:

"One weekend I got a visit from the vice-president of a large Hells Angel charter from California. He met everyone around me, my wife, girlfriends, and all the many kids who grew up in 'Dave's World.' We even went to a barbecue across the street with the square neighbors."

"After that we rode back to town so I could show off all the local night spots and how there was no business in Reno that wasn't pleased to see me and all my friends."

"So after the weekend was over, we were sitting around my pool about 2:30 Monday afternoon and I got a call on my cell phone. Because of the background noise I knew who it was right away, so I put it on the speaker phone so the HA member could here it. The voice said, 'Go outside and look up in about 45 seconds.' I replied, 'I'm sitting by the pool.' So the voice said, 'Then just look up.' We did. About 20 seconds later I hear something you never hear in Reno except during the Reno air races. The sound was unmistakable; it was two F14 Tomcats buzzing my neighborhood coming in low and fast. They came right over my backyard and then the pilot says over the cell phone, 'Hey Dave, is there anyone you don't like, give us his address. Then give him a call and tell him to go outside. Then tell him he has until sundown to get out of town.

I just laughed and told him everyone loves me. Thirty seconds later the cell phone signal was out of range."

"It couldn't have happened at a better time. The HA Vice President was impressed. How impressed? Let me tell you. A week later I got a military photo of my property taken from the spy camera on the F14 as it flew over. I took it to California to show the that vice-president."

About three years later something happened and the HA vie-president had been kicked out of the club in a bad way. It is hard to get in the club and even harder to stay in the club. So this ex-member decided to go talk to the Feds for who knows what reasons."

"Before I go any farther with this story, let me mention that as diligent as our government is on getting correct intelligence, this next bit of Intel about me was all the way off the meter."

"As I was saying, this ex-member sat down and talked to the feds a few times. One weekend I am sitting at one of the clubhouses in California and a club brother brings me some paperwork he had received from a friendly attorney. It was a transcript from one of the conversations that vice-president had with the feds. I was talked about in that transcript. That's why the transcript was shared with me. In the transcript, the ex-member had brought up the story about the F14 Tomcats. Only, this time his memory of that day's events was very different from mine. He told the feds we were having problems with some other club and I had called my Navy pilot pals and instructed them to fly over the mother charter of this other club and take some aerial recon photos of their clubhouse. How many other stories have the feds gotten wrong but run with them anyway?"

Burgess' story is probably true.

Burgess had a public profile. He maintained a website called *davesworld81*. It was about Dave's world and he was never shy about expressing his generally anti-authoritarian, patriotic and anti-government attitudes.

*****

Every Angel in the pack that day in Northern Nevada knew that every policeman they met wanted an excuse to arrest them. Arresting a Hells Angel earns cops something to brag about. What Burgess did not know was the Angel the cops wanted that day was him.

23

As is typical with the Hells Angels, the pack had been intermittently surveilled from the time it left Reno. An unknown federal agent had sent out an alert that the Freightliner motorhome, which for dramatic effect the federal agent called "the War Wagon," was headed east loaded with "drugs and guns." The alert wasn't sent to police in Nevada or Utah. The alert went to police in Wyoming.

Whoever sent out the alert knew that most of the pack and the Freightliner would pass through Wyoming before turning south. The trailer the motorhome was towing was registered in Wyoming to a company in Wamsutter named McDowell Enterprises. That trailer was what police needed to entrap Burgess because the trailer's registration expired in July.

"They are family members of a friend of mine in Reno," Dave Burgess said five years later about McDowell Enterprises. "I was carrying the trailer to his brother's business in Wyoming. I had specifically asked if the trailer had proper tags." Unbeknownst to Burgess the tags were, in fact, not "proper." They were expired. "The trailer tag had an expiration date of the month we were in. The owner of the trailer was under the assumption that the trailer tag would expire at the end of the month." But, the tag had actually expired on the first day of the month.

The pack, but not the caravan or the Freightliner, was stopped once by the Utah Highway Patrol then let go. The Freightliner wasn't stopped because the framing of Dave Burgess had already begun. Much of how Burgess was framed has been deliberately hidden in cubic acres of smoke. The evidence that can be found is circumstantial. The man who sent out the bulletin about "the War Wagon" might have been an experienced FBI agent named Edward Duffer. But whether it was Duffer or not there were other forces at work.

It is a matter of public knowledge that there is a largely secret, federal task force called the "Special Operations Division." The SOD was organized in 1994 to make cases against persons associated in some way with the Columbian drug cartels. The division combines the resources of and personnel from at least a score of federal police forces and intelligence agencies that are known to include the Federal Bureau of Investigation, the Central Intelligence Agency, the National Security Agency, the Internal Revenue Service and the Department of Homeland Security. The SOD is headquartered in an officially secret location in Virginia. Currently, the SOD

24

uses vast amounts of domestic intelligence – including but hardly limited to telephone call and email intercepts, information gathered by license plate readers, video databases, driver's license photographs and facial recognition software, all gathered as part of the Global War on Terror – to initiate criminal investigations against members of so called street gangs, outlaw motorcycle clubs, militias and other fringe groups that can be seen as domestic threats. In such investigations, the Hells Angels are usually described as a "transnational drug gang."

In 2013, the news agency *Reuters* reported that federal police who work on domestic legal cases initiated by SOD are instructed to "recreate" investigations in order to hide the involvement of the Special Operations Division and that such recreations are actually legal. "Parallel construction is a law enforcement technique we use every day" an official told the news agency. "It's decades old, a bedrock concept." What "parallel construction" means, really, is that federal polices forces routinely lie about how and why they make cases.

Reuters also quoted a "former federal agent" who said, "You'd be told only, 'Be at a certain truck stop at a certain time and look for a certain vehicle.' And so we'd alert the state police to find an excuse to stop that vehicle, and then have a drug dog search it." Illegally gathered evidence can't be introduced in court because it is illegal. But illegally gathered evidence and many dirty tricks, like burglaries, can be used to make cases. And then, with the benefit of hindsight, investigators and prosecutors can create a web of lies to explain how they know what they know, or what they think, or what they want you to think. Sometimes the lies are only lies of omission. Sometimes evidence gathered from illegal wiretaps can be attributed to anonymous sources or conversations overheard by informants or undercover agents. Sometimes evidence is simply invented, or in Dave Burgess' case, actually manufactured. That's what parallel construction is. It is a "bedrock concept." It is "how policing works."

So now, six years later, it is impossible to know whether it was SOD or some other even more secret police force that began the process of framing Dave Burgess. But something happened.

The framing of Dave Burgess began with a federal bulletin to be on the alert for a public enemy as he roamed the West in his "War Wagon." And, it can be reasonably inferred that the plan to frame Burgess was sufficiently evolved that he was not stopped in Utah. He was allowed to roll merrily on his way – oblivious to what was about to happen to him.

The Routine Traffic Stop

Burgess followed the pack off the interstate about midnight and exited onto Harrison Drive in Evanston, Wyoming. The exit is about a quarter mile from the state line and the first thing Burgess would have seen, in the dark, was a cluster of motels and gas stations. The Reno Angels spent the night at the Holliday Inn Express. The next morning, on their way to breakfast, they saw three Wyoming Highway Patrol cars parked behind JB's, a restaurant sandwiched between the Holiday Inn and the Days Inn, across the parking lot from a Quality Inn and a Chevron.

About ten, the bikers gathered around the motorhome to discuss the coming day. They saw the police watching them through the restaurant windows. The Angels were not shy about announcing who they were. Half of the motorcycles had the Angels' death head painted on the gas tank. All the bikers were wearing Hells Angel patches. "My motorcycle was in that pack with the Nevada license tag number HAMC1," Burgess said. "The cops knew exactly who we were." None of the bikers was particularly alarmed by the police staring at them. Everybody stares at Hells Angels and these Hells Angels had just awakened so they hadn't yet had time to do anything wrong.

But the soul of modern American justice is a trickster. The law isn't about right or wrong. Justice is game that rewards those who know the rules of the game best and punishes who think the law is what they learned in school. Citizens aren't usually punished because they are guilty but because they play the justice game more poorly than the police. Even when they play poorly, police usually win. They edit their accounts of what they did, what they said and what happened after the fact to conform to the letter of the law – like with "parallel construction." Cops are always given time to get their stories together. Police take courses in what to say and what not to say. Virtually every suburban mommy who has been ticketed

27

for a rolling stop and who then, in her naïveté, tried to fight the charge in court has seen how the law works.

The police had inspected the bikes and the motorhome while the Angels slept in and they had already game-planned the pretense they would use to "lawfully stop" and illegally search the chase truck. The tip of the spear was a thick, jowly, Wyoming Highway Patrol officer named Matthew Arnell. Arnell is a cop's cop. At the time he was on the Board of Directors of the Wyoming Highway Patrol Association. He would later say, many times and in many ways, that he had been told to "be on the lookout" for the "War Wagon." He would also testify several times to his "discovery" of the expired license tag.

"When me and two other troopers were going into JB's Restaurant," Arnell explained to a judge, "we were just going in to have coffee. After entering the restaurant I turned and looked out a window. And it's a big window. And I seen a motor home parked out front."

"Anything unusual about the motor home itself," a lawyer asked.

"Nothing really unusual about it, no."

"But to you, as a Wyoming highway patrolman, was there something that drew your attention to the motor home or

Some...had you received previous information about the motor home?"

"Yes. During numerous other briefings I had seen pictures of the motor home. They called it the war wagon, and it belongs to the Hells Angels."

"Could you tell us, in your training, who referred to it as the war wagon?

"Trooper Tom Adams. He's now a lieutenant."

"Tell us, please, what do you do once you see this motor home that you believe belongs to the Hells Angels motorcycle group?"

"I then went outside, looked at the vehicle, wrote down the license plate numbers to the vehicle and the trailer that was attached to it."

"Did you note anything out of the ordinary regarding the trailer?" Because the federal alert noted the easily checked Wyoming registration of the trailer, it is probably reasonable to infer that Arnell's testimony was dissembling. There is no doubt it was rehearsed.

28

"I was surprised to see Wyoming license plates on the trailer because there was Nevada license plates on the motor home."

"Anything else in regards to the trailer's license plate or licensure?"

"That the expiration sticker on the license plate showed that the plate had been expired."

"What did you do then after you made those observations, sir?"

"I looked around the parking lot some more. Seen numerous motorcycles there with the Hells Angels emblem on them on the gas tanks. Went back inside the restaurant. And, then I called my dispatch on cell phone and what we call running the plate. I checked with the dispatch on the plates, and they informed me who the owners were and that the one license plate on the trailer was expired."

"What did you do then, please?"

"Then we sat and drank coffee and I just watched the motor home out the window."

"I wonder why he didn't just walk up to us before we left the parking lot and just mention that the plate was expired," Burgess asked, rhetorically, years later. "That was when he had the most backup. The motor home had a current Nevada plate on it. The trailer had an expired plate on it. It never came up that he may have thought the trailer may have been stolen. He really was not even interested in the trailer or letting us know it had an expired plate on it before we reentered the interstate. In the parking lot having a trailer with an expired plate on it must not be against the law? You would think the courteous thing for anyone, including a policeman, to do was inform us the tag was expired."

Nine months later Arnell had an answer for that. "Well, at first there was nobody around the vehicle. But then when I did see numerous individuals out in the parking lot there around the vehicle, I didn't want to...officer safety reason. I did not want to approach the vehicle there with a lot of Hells Angels around it. For one, if something happened, I didn't want it to happen in town. If there was any shooting or anything of that nature, I didn't want anybody else getting hurt. And also I wanted to arrange to get some more backup with me so that I could stop the vehicle."

As professional policemen are trained to do, Arnell told several judges a plausible story that ignored his most significant actions and inactions. He told the truth about wanting to stop the Freightliner on the highway. He intentionally did not disclose why. The reason why had nothing to do with "officer safety" or civilian safety. Arnell is not nearly as ignorant as his words make him sound or as dull as he would like judges to think he is.

In fairness to Arnell, the Hells Angels do have a symbol called a "Dequiallo patch" that identifies members who have fought with policemen. It dates to the days when punching a policeman was a misdemeanor rather than a felony punishable with a prison sentence.

But, it would be, as a matter of fact, unprecedented for a dozen sober Angels to attack three or more Highway patrolman in the parking lot of a tourist stop at ten in the morning. It would be "conduct unbecoming a Hells Angel" because it would be incredibly stupid. The Angels would all be guilty of felonies and they would never get away – all over a minor traffic infraction. Hells Angels take the law very seriously. Because they are subject to so much harassment by the police, Angels are almost as well versed in the nuances of criminal law as cops. Besides, the Angels were on vacation. They wanted to ride 600 miles a day for four days straight because they couldn't wait to get to their big party in Arkansas.

*****

Arnell waited to stop the Freightliner until it was back on the Interstate because of a technical exception to the Fourth Amendment to the Constitution called "the vehicle exception."

The Fourth Amendment, an American right that probably seemed straightforward and unambiguous in 1791, states: "The right of the people to be secure in their persons, houses, papers, and effects, against unreasonable searches and seizures, shall not be violated, and no Warrants shall issue, but upon probable cause, supported by Oath or affirmation, and particularly describing the place to be searched, and the persons or things to be seized."

But what do those 54 words really mean?

Over the centuries, federal judges have discovered that most of the Constitution is merely a text that may be deconstructed as inventively as Jorge Luis Borges' character Pierre Menard deconstructed his *Don Quixote*. As "the fragmentary *Don Quixote* of Menard is more subtle than that of Cervantes" so the modern Constitution is more subtle than that of the Founding Fathers.

The vehicle exception to the Fourth Amendment dates to Prohibition, when forbidden alcohol, the devil's drink, was routinely transported in cars and trucks. At the time, police were local and were not part of one interconnected, quasi national police force, nor did they have two-way radios. And while a policemen went to fetch a search warrant, a rum runner might simply drive to another state outside the warrant's jurisdiction. Which might lead to the eventual sale, purchase and consumption of an alcoholic beverage. So, in a 1925 case called *Carroll versus The United States* the Supreme Court ruled that a search of a suspected bootleggers car was an "exigent search" analogous to the search of a ship at sea by the Navy: As when the American Navy intervened to prevent lawbreakers from running guns to Cuba in the 1890s. So since this great insight in 1925, police have only needed something called "probable cause" to search a car.

Probable cause is the standard stated in the Constitution for obtaining a search warrant. Because it is a legal term it has many sophistical definitions but it is generally understood, even by lawyers and policemen, as information that would cause a reasonable person to believe a crime has probably been committed. For example, a sealed liquor case might reasonably cause a silent film era policeman to believe there were probably bottles of liquor inside.

But what is a car? Is a motorhome a car?

The Supreme Court didn't get around to considering motorhomes until sixty years after *Carroll.* Even two decades after that, on the morning the Freightliner was parked in the motel parking lot in Evanston, Wyoming the law on motorhome searches was still not cut and dried. In a 1985 decision in the case *California v. Carney* the high court said a motorhome was usually a vehicle subject to a warrantless search but sometimes it might be a home. The decision overruled the California Supreme Court which had heard the *Carney* case first and had written "a motor home is fully protected by the Fourth Amendment and is not subject to the 'automobile exception,'" because "whatever expectations of privacy those travelling in an ordinary car have, those travelling in a motor home have expectations that are significantly greater."

31

The federal high court decided that what was important was that both Mercedes and Winnebagos are mobile and so, if they were transported back to 1925, both would be able to outrun the jurisdiction of a warrant; just as a gunrunner during the Spanish-American War might be able to simply slip away from the Navy in the night before a search warrant could be obtained and thus might evade the blockade of Cuba. "Historically, individuals always have been on notice that moveable vessels may be stopped and searched on facts giving rise to probable cause that the vehicle contains contraband, without the protection afforded by a magistrate's prior evaluation of those facts," the Supreme Court decreed. But the Supremes also allowed that to be subject to the vehicle exception a motorhome had to be "so situated that an objective observer would conclude that it was being used not as a residence but as a vehicle." In another words, when a motorhome is parked it might be a home. But once it is on an interstate highway there is no doubt that it is fair game for a warrantless search.

That's why Arnell waited. As he sat in the coffee shop he saw a motorhome that wasn't going anywhere. It was hemmed in and surrounded by motorcycles and for all Arnell knew someone might be inside sleeping, or eating breakfast or surfing the net. The vehicle exception as it is applied to motorhomes is unsettled so for all a legal scholar like Arnell, or whoever had told him what to do, knew the Freightliner might be occupied as the cops watched it from inside the JB's, And if that was the case any search of the Freightliner might eventually be ruled unconstitutional. And, what Arnell intended to do, what he had obviously been instructed to do, was search the "War Wagon." The point of the game wasn't to make sure everybody renewed their registration on time. The point was to conduct a warrantless search.

"Why did he wait until we had taken the trailer on the public highway," Burgess asked. "He wanted, and maybe someone else in law enforcement wanted, access to the inside of that motor home. Why? Did someone tell him that they needed access to the inside of the motor home?"

"All the luggage for the pack I was following was in the motor home," Burgess said. Including, since these were Hells Angels on vacation, almost two ounces of recreational drugs. "If the motor home was to be stopped, I knew I would be responsible for anything that was in it. The motor home

32

was traveling down the highway within the speed limit. The expired tag was a stupid mistake."

"On the other hand, I also knew the potential that the feds might have found an excuse to board the motor home once we reached the run site, but by then the luggage would have been gone. And the stash."

There were other items of police interest in the Freightliner. Sitting on a table in one of the Freightliner's two rooms was a Compaq Presario laptop computer, serial number CNFS430S7W and a portable Seagate hard drive, serial number SPLOSW17. Burgess had bought the laptop for a longtime live-in girlfriend and he had shared it with her until their breakup. For the previous four months the computer had sat on a counter in Burgess kitchen and he had brought it with him so he and other members of the Reno charter could check their email while they were on vacation. Burgess used the portable hard drive to backup his website and to store the many digital photos he took. "The computer is the one thing I was always aware of," Burgess said. "I have heard many times that all computer equipment is confiscated from clubhouses and members when the cops come in because they are all on fishing expeditions." Computer equipment is routinely seized from all motorcycle club members because police consider it to be a potential source of "gang intelligence." So it is possible that Burgess' framing began as simply an opportunity to gather "gang intelligence" on the Hells Angels.

But then, why wouldn't police have simply stopped the Freightliner in Nevada? Well for one thing, Nevada falls under the jurisdiction of the famously liberal, soft on crime, Ninth Circuit Court of Appeals. But then why not stop the Freightliner in Utah which, just like Wyoming, is under the jurisdiction of the less liberal Tenth Circuit?

*****

Arnell and the "two other troopers," who were never named, waited in the restaurant until the pack and the Freightliner drove across the street to the Pilot Flying J truck stop to fill their gas tanks. Then as the Freightliner drove back down Harrison Drive, Arnell began to follow them. "The pack pulled out onto the interstate and the motor home followed about a minute later," Burgess said. "Before we hit the end of the on ramp, one patrol car was turning onto the ramp behind us. We saw him from the cab window. He let us roll for about three miles and then he turned the red lights on us."

Shayne Waldron, Burgess' club brother from Reno, was driving. He pulled over just as the motorhome was enveloped in a trough of low hills.

The exact details of what happened next changed with virtually each retelling. Arnell's official recollections of the traffic stop were malleable and usually tailored to fit whichever government official he happened to be talking to and what those officials expected him to say. Some of Arnell's statements indicate the cat and mouse nature of the stop.

Despite his alleged concerns about "officer safety" Arnell approached the Freightliner alone, without backup, with his gun holstered and on the passenger's side of the vehicle where he was hidden from passing traffic. Without saying a word he motioned through the windshield for Waldron to get out while Burgess waited in plain sight. Arnell would later testify that he couldn't see Burgess and that he had no idea what Burgess might have been doing in the motorhome. The event was recorded by the dash camera in Arnell's cruiser from the rear of the Freightliner.

One official account reads: "On July 24, 2007, at approximately 10:00 a.m., on Interstate 80 near milepost 7.5, just east of Evanston, Wyoming Highway Patrol Trooper Matt Arnell stopped a 1999 Freightliner motorhome owned by the Defendant. The motorhome, which was being operated by Shayne Waldron, was towing a trailer that had an expired license plate. Waldron and the Defendant were the only occupants of the motor home. Upon approaching the vehicle, Trooper Arnell had Waldron exit the vehicle. When Waldron exited the vehicle Trooper Arnell smelled the odor of burnt marihuana."

That is not what happened. Waldron does not smoke marijuana. He doesn't enjoy marijuana intoxication. Nobody had smoked marijuana in the motorhome. There were no roaches in the ashtray and neither man was intoxicated in any way. But claiming to smell marijuana is one of the most common ruses police use to try to intimidate detainees and effect a technically illegal search. After the subject of marijuana came up, Waldron repeatedly offered to provide a urine sample. Arnell didn't care and none of Waldron's protestations ever made it into the official record.

34

Arnell's first account of the stop, transcribed a few hours later by a Wyoming Department of Criminal Investigation detective named Russ Schmidt, continues: "The trooper then asked Waldron about his travel plans to which Waldron replied that he and his 'brother' were traveling from Nevada to Rock Springs and from there they might go on to Denver. Waldron then gave Arnell his driver's license, insurance card, and registration. Arnell noticed that the registration for the motor home was in the defendant's name and he asked why Waldron and the defendant had different last names if they were brothers. Waldron stated he just called the defendant 'brother.'"

Arnell's first statements were contrived to imply that he had no idea that Burgess and Waldron were Hells Angels club brothers. In fact Arnell did not actually write or utter the statements attributed to him. Arnell's statements were pasted together from little lies and were intended to tell the larger lie that the traffic stop was simply routine and had not been carefully game planned. Arnell just signed his name to statements attributed to him.

"Trooper Arnell then told Waldron that the reason for the stop was the expired registration on the trailer," the first official account explains. "Waldron said he knew the plate was expired and he intended to get it renewed, which was why they were traveling to Rock Springs. Waldron then went to the trailer, retrieved the registration from inside the trailer, exited, and gave the registration to Arnell. The registration showed that the trailer was owned by McDowell Enterprises of Wamsutter, Wyoming. Arnell told Waldron that the vehicle was registered in Wamsutter and Waldron stated that was their destination, not Rock Springs. (Rock Springs is on the way from Evanston to Wamsutter.) At this point the defendant exited the motor home. After producing his identification the defendant told Arnell that he and Waldron were traveling to Arkansas for a motorcycle rally. When informed that the registration for the trailer had expired the defendant acknowledged knowing this but asked that the trooper check with the owner in Wamsutter to see if it hadn't been renewed."

"Shortly after the initiation of the traffic stop," the first official version continues, "Wyoming Highway Patrol Trooper White and Uinta County Deputy Sheriff Dave Homar arrived at the scene."

There is a Wyoming Highway Patrol Trooper named Brad White but he was probably not actually there – except possibly in spirit. His presence was probably documented in the early reports in case Trooper Arnell decided he needed another witness; someone to substantiate a lie told by one of the other participants. It is the kind of trick American police pull all the time. "There were a total of three law enforcement men and the dog at the stop in three different vehicles," Burgess insists.

According to the official account, "Deputy Homar was accompanied by his dog which had been trained and certified in the detection of controlled substances. Trooper Arnell asked Deputy Homar, to have his dog sniff the outside of the motor home while he wrote out a citation for the expired registration on the trailer."

There is another small bit of legal trickery in these couple of sentences. The federal courts have ruled that a vehicle cannot be detained in order to accomplish a drug search by a dog. But a dog can legally sniff the exterior of a vehicle while another policeman is engaged in writing a traffic citation. Compelling a motorist to wait while a cop writes a ticket is a legal detention. Compelling a motorist to wait while a dog sniffs is not a legal detention. It hardly mattered anyway. This dog drug search, like most dog drug searches, was a sham. The first account continues:

"As Deputy Homar's dog walked around the motor home it alerted, indicating that it detected the odor of controlled substances. Deputy Homar informed Trooper Arnell of the dog's alert on the motorhome. Trooper Arnell decided to search the motorhome for controlled substances based upon the dog's alert, the inconsistent travel plans provided by the Defendant and Waldron, and the smell of burnt marihuana at the outset of the traffic stop. When Arnell informed Waldron and the Defendant that he wanted to search the motor home, the Defendant said he would prefer that Arnell get a search warrant."

Burgess remembers: "When I stepped out of the motor home there was a Wyoming Highway patrol car and an SUV parked behind the trailer. There was a man with a dog walking along the trailer. About that time a dark colored sedan pulled up. The driver stayed in the car." The man in the dark colored sedan might have been Wyoming Department of Criminal Investigation Agent Russell Schmidt. Or, it might

36

have been someone else. His appearance is never mentioned in the official record, which is one of literally hundreds of lies of omission in the case.

"As we stood there on the shoulder of the road," Burgess continues, "the guy with the dog walked past the side door of the motor home. The man and the dog walked to the passenger side of the cab, turned around and walked back toward the side door. The dog continued to walk but the handler stopped by the door and pulled the dog's chain and turned the dog toward the door and pulled the chain again. The dog rose up and put his paws on the door. About this same time the Highway patrolman said he smelled pot on the other club member (Waldron). That is the first time that weed was mentioned as far as I can remember. That's a lie. The club member who was with me has never smoked weed in the entire time I have known him. He is a member of my own charter. I also had not smoked any pot that morning or the night before."

Judges never acknowledge it, but dog "alerts" are usually lies and there is no way judges can somehow not know. A professional cop named Ken Wallentine, "Chief of Law Enforcement for the Utah Attorney General" and author of the *K-9 Officer's Legal Handbook* gloats that dog sniffs are "Probable Cause on a Silver Platter." In one article on the subject, Wallentine – who double dips as a paid "law enforcement consultant," explains, "Stops for traffic violations may lead to a sniff conducted during "free time." Just as a sniff of luggage in a public place is not a Fourth Amendment search, the sniff of the exterior of a vehicle lawfully detained is not a search."

"The scope of the sniff is limited to the outside of the vehicle," Wallentine continues before citing *United States versus Sukiz-Grado* to his law enforcement readers. "'An agent may not unlawfully enter an area in order to conduct a dog search. . . . The warrantless entry of a car interior is unlawful unless there is probable cause to believe that it contains contraband.'"

"If your suspicions are aroused during the course of a traffic stop and you can articulate reasonable suspicion of drug activity, you may detain the vehicle for the arrival of a drug detection dog."

The dog in the Burgess search was a slightly goofy, female Labrador named Blitz. A federal prosecutor would later write, "Blitz (who had never given a false alert to the presence of drugs) alerted at the doors of the motor home. Trooper Arnell informed Burgess he was going to search the vehicle. Burgess said he would rather Arnell get a warrant. Nevertheless, because of the suspicions raised by Blitz's alert and the smell of marijuana, Arnell entered the motor home."

"Trooper Arnell and Deputy Homer (sic) then entered the vehicle with the K-9. Deputy Homer (sic) worked the dog on the interior of the vehicle for about one minute. Deputy Homer (sic) then told Trooper Arnell that the dog was acting confused as though it was smelling narcotics in several places and was unable to pinpoint as though the smell was everywhere."

Of course, this official account has been shamelessly tailored to conform to the exact letter of existing case law. The highest American court has visited the relationship between a dog's nose and the Fourth Amendment frequently. And, the assertion of Blitz' infallibility is at odds with consensual reality even in the magical forests where Supreme Court Justices grow. In a 2005 case called *Illinois versus Caballes* Justice David Souter dissented: "I would hold that using the dog for the purposes of determining the presence of marijuana in the car's trunk was a search unauthorized as an incident of the speeding stop and unjustified on any other ground," Souter wrote. He continued, "In *United States v. Place* we categorized the sniff of the narcotics-seeking dog as *sui generis* under the Fourth Amendment and held it was not a search. The classification rests not only upon the limited nature of the intrusion, but on a further premise that experience has shown to be untenable, the assumption that trained sniffing dogs do not err."

"At the heart both of *Place* and the Court's opinion today," Souter went on, "is the proposition that sniffs by a trained dog are *sui generis* (which is the phrase lawyers say when they mean incomparable) because a reaction by the dog in going alert is a response to nothing but the presence of contraband. Hence, the argument goes, because the sniff can only reveal the presence of items devoid of any legal use, the sniff 'does not implicate legitimate privacy interests' and is not to be treated as a search. The infallible dog, however, is a creature of legal fiction. Although the Supreme Court of Illinois did not get into the sniffing averages of drug dogs, their supposed infallibility is belied by judicial opinions describing well trained animals sniffing and alerting with less than perfect accuracy, whether owing to errors by their handlers, the limitations of the dogs themselves, or even the pervasive contamination of currency by cocaine."

Souter then cited statistics that "dogs in artificial testing situations return false positives anywhere from 12.5 percent to 60 percent of the time, depending on the length of the search."

However, even if dissenting judges here and there doubt the infallibility of dogs, courts never doubt the truthfulness of cops. The simple fact is that Blitz might very well be the Sherlock Holmes of Labrador Retrievers. But who would know and what difference would it make? No matter what Blitz did, the dog's body language was going to be interpreted by Deputy Homar on behalf of Trooper Arnell, not on behalf of some stinking Supreme Court Justice. Every judge and official who heard this carefully edited tall tale agreed that there was probable cause to believe that the Freightliner contained recreational drugs.

And, of course it did. These were Hells Angels on vacation and this was their chase truck. So of course there were drugs in the motorhome, somewhere. All Deputy Homar needed to do was tell Arnell that Blitz the infallible seemed to be alerting everywhere for Arnell to have probable cause to search everywhere. And, it is likely that neither Homar, Arnell, the invisible spirit of Trooper White nor the mystery man in the suit parked out of camera range gave a damn about the drugs because what they were really after was the laptop computer. Although, amazingly, in the official account neither Trooper Arnell, Deputy Homar nor Blitz the wonder dog saw it.

"Together with the dog, the three law enforcement officers entered the motor home" and conducted "a brief hand search of the area." Arnell would later testify under oath that the men were in the Freightliner for "about one minute" and "in several places, Deputy Homar's dog acted confused as if detecting controlled substances in several places." In a subsequent and more polished account of the warrantless search, "Deputy Homer (sic) observed K-9 Blitz alert to several areas on the interior of the vehicle. Deputy Homer (sic) observed that K-9 Blitz appeared to be in scent the entire time she was inside the vehicle due to her search patterns and intense sniffing. Deputy Homer (sic) conveyed these findings to Trooper Arnell also."

At no point in the next six years did any prosecutor, defender or judge ever utter or write that it might be possible that the search lasted less than one hundred seconds because what these crime fighters were looking for was Burgess' laptop, which as it turned out, was sitting out in the open.

The Freight Liner had front and back rooms and although he was in the motorhome only briefly and never mentioned seeing the computer Arnell did go "into the back of the motor home (where he) observed a white plastic bag by the bed, laying on the floor." Finding the K-Mart shopping bag suspicious, as Blitz the infallible Lab became "confused," as the two policemen, the dog and the spirit of Trooper White somehow avoided bumping into one another, Arnell opened the bag and found a "marijuana pipe" which he smelled and recognized as marijuana. He also recognized "trace amounts" of marijuana in the white plastic bag. By "trace amounts" Arnell seems to mean the dottle from the pipe bowl.

Making the most of his minute inside the Freightliner, Arnell "opened a cupboard" above the bed and "observed clothing." Arnell searched the clothing and found nothing. Then he found it reasonably suspicious that he had found nothing so he searched all the clothing again. Finding a suspicious piece of "tissue paper" between "two shirts" Arnell searched the tissue paper and discovered it "had something wrapped inside." He "pulled the tissue out from the shirt and unwrapped it" and "located two plastic bags containing a white powdery substance that appeared to be cocaine." The weight of the two bags was later found to be "7.2 grams and 7.0 grams including packaging."

"I then exited the vehicle," Arnell's muse, Trooper Schmitt wrote a few hours later, "and read both Mr. Waldron and Mr. Burgess the Miranda Warning and asked them both if they understood it, to which they both replied that they did. I informed them of the small wooden pipe with burnt marijuana residue and loose marijuana residue that I had found in the white bag and asked them if either one of them knew who it belonged to. Mr. Burgess then replied that it was his. I then re-entered the motor home to continue my search."

Burgess did tell Arnell it was his. As a Hells Angel, that was what Burgess was honor bound to do.

In "the top drawer of a night stand next to the bed" Arnell "located a stainless steel measuring cup containing "approximately three grams of white powder." The white powder was later determine to weigh a tenth of a gram. The same drawer also hid "a plastic bag containing a green leafy substance that looked and smelled like marijuana." The bag and its contents were later determined to weigh "10.5 grams including packaging."

"At this same time Deputy Homer informed me that he had located some marijuana in a green duffle bag behind, the driver's seat." That bag was later found to weigh "9.6 grams including packaging."

At that point Arnell impounded the Freightliner. As the mystery man parked behind the dash cam watched, Arnell "made arrangements for the vehicle to be towed to a Wyoming Highway Department shop." Waldron was then ordered into Arnell's car. "We were arrested. The other member was put in the highway patrol car and I was put in the dark sedan with the speechless driver," Burgess said. "We traveled to the local jail. The highway patrolman retrieved me from the sedan and I never saw the (silent) driver again. At least I don't think so." When asked about being interviewed by Schmitt, Burgess answers, "I remember the traffic stop, but I am not sure who Schmitt was?"

In the incident report, an account putatively written on the day of the stop, "The males were transported to the Uinta County Jail by Deputy Hutchinson and Officer Bauman," two characters who are mentioned in this drama but never seen – like convenience characters in classic television shows, like Norm's wife in *Cheers* or Mrs. Columbo.

The official accounts also contradict each other about whether Burgess and Schmitt ever had a conversation and if they did about where that conversation took place. In numerous statements under oath, government officials repeatedly asserted that Burgess and Schmitt had an incriminating conversation and in each retelling Arnell was a witness. In a federal court before a federal judge a federal prosecutor named James Anderson argued, "he (Burgess) admitted to Trooper Arnell and to Agent Russ Schmitt that he possessed the computer equipment at issue." Later Anderson told a jury, "Trooper Arnell and another investigator by the name of Russ Schmitt, who had helped with the second search, questioned the defendant."

In Burgess' eventual trial, Trooper Arnell testified, "The tow truck come, got the vehicle. I followed the tow truck and the vehicle into the state shop in Evanston, asked Trooper

White to stay with the vehicle so that nobody else could enter it, and I then met an agent from DCI, Russ Schmitt. He came over and met me in Evanston, and I spoke with him about the situation." It was also significant that Trooper White, who Burgess insists was never there, was the policeman who ensured that nothing was placed in or removed from the Freightliner.

"How was it that Russ Schmitt was called in on this stop?"

"I had already contacted the Division of Criminal Investigation, asked them if they could send an agent up to assist me with the rest of the search and whatever else may result from that search."

"Is that unusual?"

"No, that's our standard policy with the Highway Patrol."

"So you called DCI Agent Russ Schmitt. You meet. What did you and Mr. Schmitt do?"

"We then proceed to the DCI office located above the Evanston Police Department. He typed up a search warrant We were able to get that signed and then finished our search of the vehicle...."

"Now, after the search of the vehicle did you have occasion to talk with David Burgess?"

"I did."

"Where did that conversation take place?"

"At the...in a room at the Uinta County jail."

"Who was present during that conversation?"

"Myself and Agent Schmitt were both present and Mr. Burgess."

In his testimony at Burgess' trial, Schmitt described how he discovered Dave Burgess' computer. "When I walked in the motor home, I basically stayed in the front area. I recorded what everybody else was doing, took the information down on a receipt for the items we were gonna take, collected it. And at that point when I was up front there was a computer, a laptop Compaq, and an external hard drive sitting there." Schmitt's superior powers of observation may explain why he was a detective. Schmitt then explained how he said hello to Burgess.

"Subsequent to the search of the motor home did you have an opportunity to talk with David Burgess?"

"Afterwards."

42

"Where did that conversation take place?"

"It was in the Uinta County jail."

"Who was present?"

"Trooper Arnell."

"And then you had a conversation?"

"Short one."

"Could you tell us, please, did you have any discussion with Mr. Burgess about who owned the property in the motor home?"

"Um, I told him I was gonna give him a receipt showing, showing him what we took, and I asked him if everything in the motor home belonged to him. And he said, yeah, it's my motor home everything in there's mine except I've got a couple bags that I'm hauling for a couple friends."

"And did the discussion or did you discuss the computer equipment…."

"I just was showing him the receipt, and I said I…we're taking a computer, which is a laptop, and a couple external hard drives. I said we're…that's part of the list."

"And what did Mr. Burgess say, if anything?"

"He just asked if he was gonna get it back."

"And what did you tell him?"

"I said yes. I said, I said typically and being as how he was out of state, uh, usually we take it down. to the computer people, and a lot of times they'll download the hard drives and try to get it back to him as soon as we could."

Burgess says he never had the conversation Schmitt and Arnell swore took place. Burgess remembers that he read the search warrant "receipt and noticed the computer equipment was on it, I had no problem other than the hassle of having to retrieve it from the government. I knew that once they searched it they would find nothing other than back-ups of the website, *davesworld81*, the e-mail of my readers and the photos downloaded from my cameras and the photos I post online."

Arnell, Schmitt's witness, testified that the receipt for the items seized during the search "was left in the motor home."

*****

The issue of whether Burgess had a conversation with the two cops seemed unimportant at the time. Whether he ever

43

talked to Burgess or not, Schmitt officially became the lead investigator in the case as soon as the Freightliner and the bike trailer were towed back into Evanston. All of the official statements about the traffic stop were written by Schmitt. In modern legal practice, such police statements are always presumed to be true because policemen never lie. But, Schmitt did have a little history with affidavits and search warrants.

Schmitt began his law enforcement career in a little department in Green River, Wyoming and while employed there he appeared in the middle of a case any Wyoming lawyer would know. Schmitt bullied and lied his way into effecting the arrest of a Green River "drug dealer" named Richard D. Cordova. Cordova was naïve about policemen and that hindered his defense. Cordova threw himself on the mercy of the cops and wound up doing two years in the penitentiary.

The affidavit Schmitt wrote to get a search warrant in the Cordova case was blatantly untrue and it was eventually reviewed by the Wyoming Supreme Court. That court ruled that it was okay for a policeman to make things up in order to obtain a search warrant. "We agree that the affidavit in question comes uncomfortably close to violating the protections guaranteed Wyoming citizens," the court wrote about the pretense Schmitt had used to get the warrant. But "in deference to the judicial issuing officer," which is to say the judge Schmitt talked into issuing the warrant, Wyoming let Cordova's conviction stand.

In the end, the legal razor's edge that cut Cordova but not Schmitt was the fine line of "intent" – which may be even more subjective than the sense of smell. The Wyoming court presumed that Schmitt's intentions must have been good because he was a policeman. And, Cordova could not prove that Schmitt intentionally tried to violate the Constitutions of Wyoming and the United States. So the Wyoming Supreme Court ruled that even if Schmitt had lied he had not lied "deliberately" and that when he disregarded the truth he did not do so "recklessly."

Schmitt carefully worded the affidavit he created to get a warrant to search the Freightliner back in Evanston. Schmitt later stated in an evidence hearing that it was perfectly normal and reasonable to search through all the records on somebody's personal computer if you could just catch them with personal use amounts of common recreational drugs. Schmitt is hardly the only cop in the United States to say that to a judge. The legal fictions are that drug possessors are likely to be drug dealers and that drug dealers are likely to store incriminating evidence of additional drug crimes on their computers.

Defense attorneys know the ruse. A defender in Little Rock named John Wesley Hall writes: "I am seeing computer searches added virtually all the time into drug search warrant applications by state officers, not so much by federal, and this has been going on here for about three years. Apparently some police training…got them on to this, so they uniformly allege that "in affiant's experience, drug dealers keep records on computers," as if the run of the mill street dealer uses Quicken or Excel to keep a profit-loss statement."

In "Arnell's" search warrant affidavit, Schmitt claimed, "Based upon training and experience, your Affiant knows that persons involved in trafficking or the use of narcotics and dangerous drugs often keep photographs of coconspirators or photographs of illegal narcotics in their vehicle…. Your Affiant knows that paraphernalia for packaging, cutting, weighing, and using is commonly kept in the vehicle of the drug trafficker. Subjects involved often keep pay-owe sheets, and receipts of customers and subjects also involved with drug trafficking keep weapons to protect there (sic) narcotics and drug proceeds."

Who would possibly believe that? A Wyoming Circuit Court Judge named Michael Greer believed that. He issued the search warrant. Readers can decide whether Schmitt is a liar or not. This is from the evidentiary hearing.

"And why did you think that it was important to take that computer and that hard drive that you saw right there?"

"Well, 'cause, you know, we'd already found cocaine and marijuana, and, you know, there's a good chance that, one, it would have pictures of coconspirators or other people or e-mails of drug trafficking or the person that drove the vehicle itself standing there with drugs to show that, yes, this person is into drugs or, I mean, several reasons."

"So photographs certainly?"

"Yes, sir."

"Names or information pertaining to other people that might be engaged in illegal activity?"

"E-mails."

"E-mails that might show or relate to illegal activity relating to these controlled substances or controlled substances; is that correct?"

"Yes. In a lot of them we've confiscated several computers where they are actually downloading things on how to make methamphetamine, recipes. And I think that…to be honest, I believe that's…I know there wasn't methamphetamine found at this, but that kind of started the trend for taking computers two years ago because of the downloading of methamphetamine recipes, and then it just kind of went from there to be more mainstay all the time."

So Schmitt and Arnell, and probably some other people who were not ghosts like Trooper White, tossed Burgess' motorhome a second time.

Officially, Arnell's roadside search, when he unfolded all of Burgess' and Waldron's shirts twice and went through their socks and their underwear was a "cursory search." Officially Arnell never saw the computer and the portable hard drive just sitting there on a table. Officially, Agent Schmitt did not discover the Compaq laptop and the Seagate hard drive until after they obtained a warrant to "search" for computer equipment. During the second search, conducted in private, while the phantom Trooper White stood guard outside, Schmitt and Arnell found a third piece of computer equipment. They found a broken Maxtor portable hard drive that Burgess had left at home in Reno in a drawer.

Arnell would later testify that he, not Schmitt, had discovered the laptop.

"Second search of the vehicle revealed another small plastic baggie with some white powder in it that I suspected to be cocaine, and then the original computer and hard drive that I had located beside the bed, and then I also located another hard drive up underneath a couch," Arnell swore.

"Tell us about that, please, that second hard drive that you just mentioned."

"I was on my hands and knees more or less in the living area completing the search, and I looked up under a couch. There were some slots up under the couch where you could see up under there, and I could see the hard drive up under, under there. Was able to get my hand up through the slot, grab a hold of the hard drive. And when I tried to pull the hard drive out, I was having some difficulty getting it out of there. My watch hung up on the slot I was reaching through. I had to reach through with my right hand, undo my watch, finish removing that hard drive."

Years later, Burgess said, "I only took one hard drive with me. It was always a mystery how that other hard drive got in my motor home. And another oddity, the hard drive that was found under my sofa in the motor home looked just like an old hard drive that I owned but my old hard drive had malfunctioned and froze up, so I bought a new one. I backed up my web-site every week, that is why I owned the hard drives in the first place. Also I downloaded all the photos I took at club events to the hard drive. That is another reason I would not have anything on the hard drive I wouldn't want club Brothers or family members to see. The government never mentioned that the old hard drive was frozen."

Schmitt would later say he collected all three items "as evidence, put them on the receipt, and then when I got everything together had Al Ehrhardt. who is from Cheyenne with the DCI, I just had him transport it down to Cheyenne instead of putting it in my evidence vault. Schmitt turned the computer and two hard drives over to Ehrhardt that afternoon. Elvin "Al" Ehrhardt was the Wyoming Department of Criminal Investigation "authority" on "gangs." It was his job to gather and interpret "intelligence" about motorcycle clubs.

In his testimony at trial, Ehrhardt alludes to his participation in the search of the Freightliner. "Once the search had completed and I was preparing to come back to Cheyenne, I received a laptop and two external hard drives to bring back to deliver to our ICAC unit for a forensic review." Ehrhardt kept meticulous notes about the transportation of the computer equipment. The notes are considered infallible proof that the chain of custody of the seized items was secure.

"Received from Russ Schmitt at 2030 hours, 7/24 of 2007, at DOT shop, Evanston. Transported to Cheyenne Department of Criminal Investigation headquarters, 0130 hours. Locked up in Intel safe number 2, 7/25 of 07. 0900 hours, 7/25 of 07 checked items, still secure. Was planning to transfer items to ICAC for analysis, however ICAC out. Locked back in Intel safe number 2 0930 hours, 7/25 of 07. Will transfer on 7/26 of 07."

"And did, in fact, did you transfer them on that day, or did you get them taken care of on the 25th," a prosecutor asked Ehrhardt.

Who replied, "They actually returned earlier than what I thought, so I was actually able to take them over to them on the 25th."

The acronym ICAC represents the Wyoming Internet Crimes Against Children Team.

*****

Ehrhardt handed the computer and the two drives to an ICAC Agent named Randall Huff.

Huff was asked, "I'd like to call your attention to July 25th of 2007. On that particular day did you have occasion to come into possession of certain computer equipment from an individual known as Al Ehrhardt?"

"I did..... He came into our office, which is located here in Cheyenne up on North Yellowstone, uh, brought in some evidence that he said that the southwest investigators, Division of Criminal Investigation agents, were working and they wanted some computer forensic work done on those items of evidence. One was a laptop, and I believe it was two external hard drives.... I logged them in, put them into our secure evidence holding facility located at our premises there on North Yellowstone."

"You say a secure, a secure evidence facility."

"It's a room that's locked. Uh, and also the building is locked, doors are locked and, uh, has an alarm security system."

"Did you do the intake?"

"I did the intake, yes."

"And who was assigned to the investigation?"

That man was Agent Scott Michael Hughes.

The next day the Denver *Post* ran a brief notice about the "Hells Angels Bikers Arrested in Wyoming." The story described what would become the skeleton of the criminal case. "Wyoming Highway Patrol troopers noticed a trailer with an expired Wyoming registration tag." "During the traffic stop, a small amount of marijuana was found." "Troopers obtained a search warrant for the motor home and found about 14.9 grams of cocaine." Also, the *Post* reported, the motorhome was "known as the 'War Wagon,'"

Waldron and Burgess quickly bailed out. Burgess was used to police harassment but he was worried about picking up a felony charge for drug possession.

48

He didn't give his missing laptop and his Seagate portable hard drive much thought until an FBI Swat team burst into his home, on a quiet street named Mayberry, two months later, on October 25th. The FBI seized all the rest of Dave Burgess' computer equipment and some of his photographic equipment

The Reno *Gazette* reported that the FBI remained "mum" about the raid. "We are here executing a search warrant and that's really all we can say," an FBI Agent named Bill Woerner told the paper. The *Gazette* reported that "Agents, many carrying assault rifles and wearing bullet-proof vests, also declined to say what they found during the search of the home Thursday."

But, Woerner was less obtuse with Burgess. The FBI was looking for evidence related to the manufacture, possession and distribution of child pornography. According to Burgess, Woerner said "if I did not agree to get the Hells Angels Motorcycle Club involved in some criminal adventure they would make sure to make me look so bad that even my brothers in the Hells Angels would disown me, and that I would spend the next 20 years in prison branded as a pedophile."

The Family Owned Business

Dave Burgess inherited his status as an enemy of the state – as a man who was asking for it and deserved to be framed. He inherited most of his enemies. He inherited the source of his wealth.

Dave's aunt was Sally Burgess. That was his original sin. Although, to this day many women in Nevada remember Sally had a heart of gold. Sometimes she called herself Jesse Sally Burgess. Sometimes she was Sally Conforte. For decades Sally and her husband Joe Conforte ran the most successful and profitable business in sparsely populated Storey County, Nevada, which begins about eight miles east of Reno.

Sally did most of the work. Joe, who is sometimes remembered as an immigrant success story, took most of the credit.

Joe Conforte was born in Augusta, Sicily about halfway between Catania and Syracuse and he immigrated to Boston with his father and stepmother in 1936. Although his family had fled the old regime, Joe remains an admirer of Benito Mussolini to this day. "Hey, Mussolini wasn't a bad guy," he argued in 1991. "His only mistake was joining up with Hitler."

Joe's early history is misty. He ran away from home as a teenager and he may or may not have served in the American Army in the Pacific during World War II. He was 19 when the war ended. He became a naturalized American citizen in 1946. He claimed to have spent time on Guam. He was a cab driver in Oakland in 1950, when the Bay area was still crawling with soldiers, sailors and Marines, and that was how Joe became a pimp.

Joe knew the addresses of all the best whorehouses – which were the ones that paid him a commission. A couple of years later he was a pimp in northern Nevada, where the laws regulating sin were few and capriciously enforced. He opened his own whorehouse near Carson City in 1955. He called it the Triangle Ranch because it was on land that occupied conjoined

50

bits of three counties. The women worked in trailers and when the law in one county would shake him down Joe would just hook the trailers up to a tractor and pull them fifty yards or so into one of the other two counties.

Sally Burgess, who was ten years older than Joe, had made her way in the world as a whore. She opened her own whorehouse in Fallon, Nevada in 1955. Later that year she opened another house in Wadsworth and that's where she met Joe. The next year, when her little nephew David in San Diego was four years old, she went partners with Conforte. She was smart enough to let Joe front the business and handle the politicians.

In the 1950s, the women in Joe and Sally's houses were paid $10 for a 30 minute date. The house cut was 50 percent. The women worked in 12-hour-shifts and anal sex and kissing on the mouth were strictly prohibited. Reno cab drivers got a 10 percent commission. "I've never been ashamed of the business," Joe would say 30 years later. "You are never going to eliminate prostitution. If you are going to have it anyway, then isn't it better to have it controlled?" The argument over whether prostitution should be legal continues to this day. Libertarian Nevada is the only state that tolerates it.

Joe became increasingly flamboyant as the Triangle Ranch prospered. Most people loved him. Dave Burgess inherited some of his flamboyance from his uncle.

Joe Conforte became famous for handing out cigars wrapped in twenty dollar bills to policemen. There was no law against prostitution in Nevada but the state has always had both moralistic and corrupt sides that the tourists never see. The state has a strong Mormon presence. The first white settlement in Nevada was Mormon Station near Lake Tahoe about 50 miles south of Reno. In the days after World War II many Nevada natives thought prostitution violated God's law and that open prostitution violated the law of common decency.

In 1959, when Joe was 33, he was "banned" from Reno by the recently elected Washoe County District Attorney, and later Nevada State Senator, William Raggio. Raggio eventually became the longest serving state senator in Nevada history. The former College of Education Building at the University of Nevada at Reno is now and forevermore will be called the William J. Raggio Building. And, all of Raggio's celebrated career was the fruit of a dispute between Raggio and

51

Joe Conforte. To a surprising extent, the framing of Dave Burgess grew out of the dispute between those two powerful men.

Raggio and Conforte were both Sicilian and the argument between them was basically a dispute over who was most masculine. Raggio would later say: "Conforte thought he was bigger than the law, and so it became a test of who was going to run the county – him or the district attorney. That's how it grew into what you might call a 'contest of wills.' If he had been a guy running a brothel in another county, who didn't do all that, he probably would not have been bothered by the authorities. However, his presence was a violation of the law because he was obviously a pimp."

Raggio decided to teach Conforte a lesson. He ordered police to arrest Conforte anytime he was spotted in Reno. At the time Raggio denied he had ever given "explicit instructions" to run Conforte out of town but years later he admitted he had. He recalled, "that was often complicated because many members of the law enforcement community considered him a friend and refused." Raggio's logic was simple. Conforte owned a whorehouse and he was usually accompanied by a whore so he was a pimp. And, as far as Raggio was concerned pimps were vagrants by definition. So it wasn't long before Raggio overcame the objections of his cigar smoking cops and managed to get Conforte arrested for vagrancy twice in one night.

That infuriated Joe who was determined to exact revenge. A few days later Conforte sent a 17 year old prostitute named Jacqueline Hinson to find Raggio at one of his favorite watering holes; a place called the Corner Bar in the old Riverside Hotel next to the county courthouse. Raggio enjoyed the girl's company and he bought her a couple of drinks.

It was legal at that time in Nevada for a district attorney to maintain a private practice and Raggio had a little law business on the side. In the fifties, Reno was famous for "quickie divorces" and all the lawyers in town made money from that. As they drank, Hinson told Raggio that she was 22, that she had come to Reno for her divorce and that she didn't have much money but she really hated her husband and she would do anything for a good divorce lawyer. So Raggio and the underage girl who looked older than she was went upstairs to her room to discuss her imaginary case.

Five days later Joe Conforte asked Bill Raggio to meet him at his lawyer's office. Joe's lawyer was a man named Frank Peterson and Conforte thought that might be a safe place although he remained worried that the conversation might be bugged. He frisked Raggio before they began negotiating. Raggio played along and frisked Conforte in return. Of course, Peterson's office was bugged. Raggio was the District Attorney. He had had a local judge named Grant Bowen order Peterson's office wiretapped. So the wiretap was legal and the entire conversation between the two men was recorded.

After a moment of small talk Conforte told the DA that because so many people in Northern Nevada were inclined to turn to Joe for help he had heard from Hinson's mother. They were both men of the world and it was really none of Joe's business what Raggio had done to a poor and wayward girl, but Joe had, in order to maintain his good name and keep his standing in the community, promised the mother that he would try to "work something out." When the conversation turned blunt Conforte told Raggio, "I want this charge against me dropped and I want a public apology right there in the court room." If Raggio didn't acquiesce Conforte promised to have Raggio charged with providing liquor to a minor and statutory rape.

Raggio laughed, "Who do you think you're going to get to do that?"

To which the always surprising Joe replied, "The attorney general would do it. He'd love to do it. It would make him governor." At the time the Nevada Attorney General was a man named Roger Foley.

"You mean you have Roger in your pocket, too?"

"I have something on George," Joe explained. George F. Foley, Roger Foley's younger brother was the district attorney of Clark County which surrounds Las Vegas. Both of those Foleys were the sons of Judge Roger T. Foley, for whom the Foley Federal Building in downtown Las Vegas is named.

The conversation was profanity laced and mostly cordial. Eventually Raggio wanted Conforte to reassure him that Joe would keep quiet about the potential scandal. "All I want is to be left alone," Conforte said. "I want to be friends. I want to be treated like a human being,"

Raggio told Conforte he wanted to think it over and arranged, by his accounts, to meet Conforte in Virginia City. Neither man attended that meeting. Instead Raggio sent

53

sheriff's to the brothel in Lyon County and had Dave Burgess' uncle arrested there for extortion. Joe was quickly sentenced to two years in state prison and four months after Raggio had accompanied Jacqueline Hinson upstairs to her room at the Riverside, he declared the Triangle Ranch a "public nuisance" and watched as a company from the Reno Fire Department burned the place to the ground.

It was Joe's first jail sentence. Sally waited for him. They married when he was released. And, within a month they were both in trouble with the law again. This time, in a federal drama that would recur over and over and would eventually be bequeathed to Dave Burgess, Joe was charged with income tax evasion. It was his first encounter with federal justice. There is little doubt he was fudging his income taxes and he pled guilty in June 1963. But after he was released in December 1965 Joe and Sally bounced right back.

While Joe was on ice, a man named Richard Bennett had opened a brothel in Storey County. Bennett called it the Mustang Bridge Ranch. The whorehouse was named for the bridge over the Truckee river that connected it to the Lincoln Highway. But Bennett lacked Joe and Sally's experience in the whore business and, coincidentally, he suffered an unfortunate series of misfortunes after Joe was released. Someone kept setting his whorehouse on fire. Then some scoundrel blew up the Mustang Bridge so customers couldn't get to Bennett's place. Joe and Sally made Bennett an offer in 1967, took the useless brothel off his hands and immediately rebuilt the bridge.

Joe, or Sally – who was less voluble and charismatic than her husband but who might have been the more intelligent – had a plan for dealing with local politicians. When the Confortes bought Bennett's place, 200 square mile Storey County had fewer than 600 residents and less than half of them were eligible to vote. So Joe, or Sally, quickly deduced that they could control most local elections by delivering a mere 150 votes. Joe accomplished that by moving trailers into a housing development that adjoined the Mustang and renting them out at bargain rates to people who were down on their luck.

Fourteen years later, when the population of Storey County had soared to 2500 with almost 1500 registered voters, Joe told the Los Angeles *Times*: "I am not going to lie to you . . . I want to keep (the residents) happy and for political reasons. I go around the trailer park and tell the people: 'Look, you've got two candidates. Now, I think this one is pro prostitution, this one is not, and I would like you to vote for this one.' I am not going to discount the fact that I control more than 20 percent of the vote in Storey County. But where is the law against that?"

Compared to nearby Reno, Storey County was impoverished. It was mostly sagebrush and range without a single casino or hotel. The misfortunes at the Mustang Bridge Ranch were a drain on public services. A local judge ordered Conforte to close his bagnio and ordered Joe to pay the County $1,000 a month for five months to pay for the police patrols that would ensure the Mustang stayed closed. Joe cheerfully paid the county the money every month. He was generous with the cops who were supposed to make sure the brothel was closed. So, because government and law are essentially corrupt, the Mustang Bridge Ranch managed to stay open. And, Storey County came to depend on Joe's monthly payments and his generosity. Everybody knew the arrangement was hypocritical.

After three years, the county district attorney told the county commissioners that Storey County couldn't take anymore of Joe and Sally's money without passing an ordinance authorizing the payments. And, that was how, in December 1970, the Mustang Bridge Ranch became the first licensed brothel in the United States. A few months later, the Confortes shortened the name of their family business to the Mustang Ranch and it became a symbol of the "sexual revolution." Joe appeared in *Look* the next June and in November 1972 he was on the cover of *Rolling Stone*.

Joe and the Mustang Ranch became lightening rods and the Confortes became rich. For many Americans, the Mustang Ranch represented everything that was going wrong with the country and the Confortes began to make new enemies. Joe developed a reputation as the godfather of northern Nevada and his words grew in power. When he mentioned that he was thinking of opening a whorehouse in Las Vegas the big casinos lobbied the Nevada legislature to pass a law that prohibited brothels in counties with more than 200,000 people. Which at the time meant that only Clark County was forbidden by the new law from legalizing houses of ill repute.

In 1976 Sally began managing Argentine heavyweight fighter Oscar Bonavena. Bonavena was most famous for going

14 rounds and two minutes with Muhammad Ali before being technically knocked out. Sally and Oscar had a sexual affair. The affair eventually became the subject of an astoundingly unpopular, Taylor Hackford movie named *Love Shack*. Hackford's wife, Helen Mirren portrayed Sally. Joe Pesci played Joe. And, the movie ended the same way the affair ended, with one of Joe's guards gunning down the big fighter. The movie portrayed the incident as a crime of passion. In 2008 Joe told television station *KTVN*, the *CBS* affiliate in Reno, that he was never jealous.

"I gotta tell the truth," Joe claimed. "Everybody is gonna call me a villain after this, but it was a hidden relief for me. Now I don't have to take her to town every night and I don't have to get in bed with her everyday you know? Here's a woman that's eleven years older than me. I was going with a few girls at the same time." Joe remembered it was all about business. According to Joe, Bonavena "told everybody 'from now on, I'm gonna be the big boss of the Mustang Ranch.' That was a little bit too much."

The next year the Reno *Gazette* won its only Pulitzer Prize for a series of scathing editorials about Joe. The Mustang Ranch had become a convenient symbol for both corrupt local politics and a raging national debate over morality and sex. In response to the *Gazette* editorials a grand jury was convened to look at the Confortes but it was dismissed without returning an indictment. Then, eleven months after Bonavena died, Joe's old nemesis, the Internal Revenue Service charged the Confortes with ten counts of tax evasion. They were both fined $10,000. Sally got a suspended sentence and Joe got five years. They appealed but the end was drawing near for Joe and Sally.

*****

Dave Burgess worked at the Mustang off and on starting in 1974, when he was 22. He started as a handy-man and worked as a bartender, cashier and "bridge man. Really the job was "security guard." The principal duty of a bridge man was to make sure nobody blew up the bridge from the interstate to the Mustang – as had happened to the previous owner.

Burgess version of events is, "After a few years and about six different managers, I started going to my Uncle Joe and telling him I could run that place way better than those lame managers he kept hiring. He would just laugh and tell me to get back to work."

Something closer to the truth is that Joe's appeal didn't go well and Dave was family. Contingencies had to be prepared. The Mustang filed for bankruptcy. Joe needed somebody he could trust. Joe's own son was a drug addict and his addiction had ravaged his brain. So on March 6, 1979 Dave Burgess remembers, "My Uncle Joe called me up to his house. I thought I might be in some sort of trouble because going to see Uncle Joe was like going to see the Godfather. Even back then, I was ready for anything. Well, it turns out, he was ready to give me a chance at managing the largest legal brothel in America. I was 27 years old at the time." Burgess met the lawyers and became the Mustang's official trustee. That was how he became an official co-conspirator of the Godfather of Northern Nevada.

He began to learn the whorehouse business and he settled into life in Reno. He moved into a house "a couple doors down" from a couple named Jay and Yvonne Regas and their children. He became friends with their oldest son, Troy.

Joe Conforte lost his appeal in 1980 and deeded his interest in the Mustang to Sally. Two months later she deeded Joe's interest in the Mustang back to him, pending bankruptcy reorganization.

Joe forfeited a $240,000 bail and moved to a penthouse in Rio overlooking the beach at Ipanema. It was the beginning of a decades long battle over the Mustang's assets. It was also the beginning of Dave Burgess' decades long education in the law and the first flowering of his doomed life. Burgess was clearly not his Uncle Joe although he obviously admired Conforte's flair. David was not a hustler. He had the soul of an artist. Managing the Mustang allowed him the leisure to pursue his interest in photography. He loved gardens and flowers. But he inherited his Uncle Joe's enemies – both in and out of the government – so he was compelled to begin his informal education in American justice.

Late in 1982 Joe opened a Swiss bank account in the name of Jose C. Montoya. The IRS was able to monitor the account and would later state that Joe made numerous transactions through it.

The world at large might have comprehended the Mustang Ranch symbolically but the people connected to it always understood the Mustang was a pot of gold. Nobody to this day knows how lucrative the Mustang was but it obviously put enough money in Joe Conforte's pocket that he could eat a small fortune in penalties and relocate to paradise. Joe had issues with the IRS mostly because that Service, like all the rest of all America's government, is made of men not ideals. Some men detested Conforte because they thought he was a bad man in a bad business. Other men wanted Conforte to pay them off.

For decades, the real tax issue for Conforte, and later Dave Burgess, was whether the whores who worked at the Mustang were employees or independent contractors. In the early days of the ranch, Joe required the women to have pimps because he thought that arrangement would encourage the women to make more money. Joe eventually dropped that requirement but the women who seduced and negotiated and quickly pleased were still virtually prisoners of their job. When you worked at the Mustang Ranch you could only spread your legs for the Mustang. You couldn't meet a trick at the Mustang bar, work out a deal then go into town later to meet him and keep all the money for yourself. So the women were stuck in the house for weeks at a time. They needed permission to go into Reno and when they did they had to hire a chaperone. Chaperoning whores was one of the odd jobs Dave Burgess did for his uncle. The women split their income from each sexual encounter evenly with the house and they were required to buy their cosmetics, clothes and other supplies from Joe and Sally. It was a system they created a lot of jobs for security guards, maintenance men and even an in-house Avon Lady. Joe told the government the women were working for themselves so he never withheld income taxes or social security taxes from the women. The IRS insisted that the women were clearly working for Joe and so he should be withholding taxes. That was most of the tax issue. The Mustang was so profitable that everybody wanted a bigger share. Local politicians and cops wanted more. The IRS wanted more. And occasionally someone with the power to push his weight around would object that selling sex was just plain wrong.

Two years after Joe left the country, Storey County convened another grand jury to investigate who Joe might have bribed and how much he paid. Eventually, that gave Joe leverage in his case. The grand jury concluded that Joe held "unusual influence and power" in Storey County. It named the district attorney and sheriff who had investigated Bonavena's death but it didn't indict anybody. Unless Joe cooperated, nobody was going to be indicted. That's why Joe traded Rio for Reno in 1983. Once he was home Joe confessed that he had paid a judge named Harry Claiborne $85,000 in bribes. He agreed to testify against Claiborne and in return Joe's prison sentence was reduced from 20 years to 18 months. The Claiborne case ended in a mistrial, probably because the jury didn't believe Joe and possibly because Joe already had what he wanted and he didn't care whether anybody believed him or not. When Joe got out of prison, again, he immediately went back into the brothel business, again. His first move was to try to sell the Ranch. And, of course, every move he made was watched very carefully.

As Joe was negotiating his plea deal, Dave Burgess was supervising construction on a second brothel a hundred yards from the original Mustang. That cathouse was called Mustang Two. But even two whorehouses couldn't make enough money to pay off a growing tax debt. Burgess started construction on a third brothel, about two hundred yards west of the Mustang Two in 1983. It was to be a separate business from the other two houses. It would belong to Dave. And, in September 1984 Burgess quit the Mustang and opened his own place. He called it the Old Bridge Ranch and it was also very carefully watched.

By then Dave was dating Ingrid Regas, his neighbor's daughter. He remained close friends with Ingrid's brother Troy Regas and he became friends with Troy's younger brother Sohn. Dave hired their Dad, Jay Regas, to run the bar at the Old Bridge. Jay's wife Yvonne also helped out around the place. The Regas were and remain a physically beautiful and all American family. In the 80s they most resembled the fictional Partridge family. One of the daughters would later date John Ascuaga, Jr. whose father had founded the casino that would later contain the Hells Angels and Vagos shootout. Dave Burgess encouraged his in-laws to think of the Old Bridge as their family business and they did. Troy eventually worked there. Jay would later write, "We are a close knit family who operate a family business where we all work together...a family-owned legal-brothel in Nevada."

Dave and Ingrid, a knockout blonde, a former Budweiser girl with her mother's curly hair but blonde like her brother Sohn, were married in 1986. And they loved each other but they did not get along as husband and wife. They did get along well as business partners. Although Ingrid was younger than David she was certainly the more practical of the two. From early in their marriage she actually ran the whorehouse which, once he was out from under his uncle's shadow, allowed Dave Burgess to imitate all the things Nevada had loved about his Uncle Joe. Starting in 1984 David gave away 800 turkeys every year to needy families. He paid dental and medical bills for the indigent, bought school children clothes, paid rents and bought cars.

There was more drama in the early 90s. Joe started moving money around between his Swiss bank account and a corporation called Mustang Properties. That September, the IRS seized the Mustang, considered running it, then locked the doors and sold it to Mustang Properties for $1.5 million.

David's in-laws, Jay and Yvonne, split up. Then David and Ingrid separated. Dave left Reno and moved to Oakland to begin the long process of becoming a Hells Angel. Ingrid stayed in Reno and ran the Old Bridge Ranch. Then Jay and Troy Regas and dozens of other people were indicted by a federal grand jury in Reno for selling drugs.

Jay spent a year in jail before the beginning of a year long trial. The indictment against David's father-in-law was superseded five times over a period of two years as various participants made plea deals and told new stories to prosecutors. The government alleged that Jay had started selling large amounts of cocaine and methamphetamine in 1982 and kept at it for a decade. Prosecutors called it the "Regas Drug Organization."

What followed was the legal version of musical chairs. Various defendants fell all over each other to win immunity by testifying against someone else. It is still a basic strategy in federal criminal cases. Prosecutors don't care about getting the right villain. They care about getting a memorable one. Jay's nickname was "Cowboy." To this day Dave Burgess remains sincerely convinced that his father-in-law was punished because of his association with the Old Bridge Ranch and the Old Bridge's association with Joe Conforte. If the feds couldn't get Joe they could at least get Cowboy Regas.

The charges against Jay and Troy Regas varied from the glamorous to the fantastic. Jay was accused of distributing eight pounds of cocaine at the Beverly Wilshire Hotel in Beverly Hills. The total sales of the Regas Organization were said to amount to $160 million and if that was true Jay was even better at making money invisible that Joe Conforte had been because other than a few pieces of relatively inexpensive Western Art, nobody had any idea where Jay put the money. One of the witnesses, a destitute, undocumented Mexican immigrant said Jay tried to sell him 300 kilos of cocaine in a Chinese restaurant. Another witness claimed to know who was responsible for an unsolved string of serial murders.

It is plausible that sometime during the *Miami Vice* years, Jay and Troy sold some amount of cocaine. One of the stories the government told was that Troy, on behalf of his father, sold a drug dealer named Rene Herrera four ounces of cocaine in the Reno Hilton in 1986. Then when Herrera did not pay for the cocaine three men named Perry Joseph Gilmartin, David Wayne Hogle, and Clayton Ross kidnapped the debtor and took him to a house where a fourth man named Bubba Garfinkle beat Herrera with a flashlight as Troy watched. It is also plausible that Jay and Troy had nothing to do with the drug deal or the beating. The two have always argued that they were innocent and that they were the only two defendants out of dozens who actually had jobs – working at David's brothel. Jay's seizable assets only amounted to $3,000. Maybe Cowboy Regas buried his lost fortune in a hole in the desert.

As more and more defendants earned lenient sentences by testifying that Cowboy Regas did it, Yvonne Regas began to panic. Both Jay and Troy faced 450 years in prison and Yvonne was convinced her ex-husband and her son had been framed. She was a Nevadan and she had libertarian tendencies. During the trial, searching for something she could do to help, she learned about the idea of "jury nullification" – in which juries may choose to acquit a defendant when it thinks the defendant is simply guilty of breaking a bad law. The concept has a long history in the United States. Before the Civil War, northern juries often returned not guilty verdicts in cases against defendants who actually did harbor runaway slaves and were then prosecuted for violating the Fugitive Slave Act of 1850. During Prohibition, juries sometimes acquitted defendants who had actually broken the law against selling alcoholic beverages.

Yvonne Regas acquired information from a Montana non-profit corporation called the Fully Informed Jury Association. The Association believes "the primary function of the independent juror is not, as many think, to dispense punishment to fellow citizens accused of breaking various laws, but rather to protect fellow citizens from tyrannical abuses of power by the government." She got a brochure from the Association titled "Your Jury Rights: True or False" and she had copies made at her own expense. The brochure, which is still available from the Association, contains statements such as:

"In a trial by jury, the judge's job is to referee the event and provide neutral legal advice to the jury, properly beginning with a full explanation of a juror's rights and responsibilities. But judges only rarely 'fully inform' jurors of their rights, especially their right to judge the law itself and vote on the verdict according to conscience. In fact, judges regularly assist the prosecution by dismissing prospective jurors who will admit knowing about this right – beginning with anyone who also admits having qualms with the law."

For three days, Yvonne Regas and a friend put that brochure under the windshields of cars in the courthouse parking lot. Eight months later, after a lengthy and expensive investigation, the same prosecutor who had charged her husband and her son charged Yvonne Rigas with three criminal counts: "Conspiracy to Commit Offenses Against the United States, to-wit, to Obstruct the Due Administration of Justice and to Corruptly Endeavor to Influence and Impede a Petit Juror or Petit Jurors and Aiding and Abetting; Obstruction of the Due Administration of Justice and Aiding and Abetting; and to Corruptly Endeavor to Influence, Intimidate or Impede a Petit Juror or Petit Jurors."

Yvonne Regas faced two years in prison and a $30,000 fine. The prosecutor, Ron Rachow, told the Las Vegas *Review Journal*, "Her attorney may think this is a First Amendment issue, but not all speech is constitutionally protected." The charges promoted a small furor in Nevada and within a week Yvonne Regas was offered her own plea deal. The court would dismiss the charges if she accepted a "pre-trial diversion," she agreed to do 100 hours of "community service" and she promised to never again publically advocate for jury nullification. She took the deal. In federal justice the smart move is almost always to take the deal.

In the meantime Troy had been found guilty of two of the 38 charges against him and he was sentenced to five years in a federal prison for conspiracy to distribute illegal drugs and participating in a "continuing criminal enterprise." Jay was sentenced to consecutive life sentences without the possibility of parole. Manuel Noriega, the former dictator of Panama through whose country any drugs Jay Regas sold would have passed, was tried about the same time in federal court. Noriega was sentenced to 30 years and he was released after doing a little more than half of that.

*****

And, still the drama surrounding Dave Burgess' life continued to swoop and twist like a kite in March. Joe Conforte fled to Brazil for good in 1991. Sally Burgess died the next year.

Throughout the 90s the Department of Justice continued to pursue bankruptcy fraud and tax evasion charges against Conforte. A federal grand jury indicted both Joe and his lawyer Peter Perry. Perry pleaded innocent and made a deal with prosecutors to testify against Joe. The IRS filed a $16 million tax lien against Conforte and the corporation that then owned the Mustang. In 1998 the U.S. Attorney for the District of Nevada filed criminal charges against Conforte, two corporations and three former employees of the Mustang Ranch. The next year U.S. Marshalls closed the Mustang for good and seized all of the brothel's tangible and intangible assets including the name "Mustang Ranch." An IRS spokesman named James Collie announced that this time there was "no intention of the Government to operate it as a brothel."

The Old Bridge endured and Burgess' ambition to become a Hells Angel endured. For government investigators and prosecutors and for IRS officials the Old Bridge Ranch became *Moby Dick*. The same investigators, prosecutors and officials who had hounded Joe Conforte to his penthouse in Rio thought Burgess was thumbing his nose at legal authority, which was at least partly true.

David returned from Oakland and together with Troy, who was free on appeal, and Troy's younger brother Sohn, formed a club called the Renegades Motorcycle Club in 1994. David was President. The Renegades became what is called a "hang around" club for the Angels and then a "prospect club."

"After a few years the feds got onto what I was trying to do," Burgess said, "and they came to me and told me that

63

there would never be a chapter of the Hells Angels in the state of Nevada." In 1998, as criminal charges were being brought against Uncle Joe, the Renegades patched over and officially became the first Hells Angels charter in the Silver State. The New Angels charter would eventually buy Joe Conforte's house at auction and use it as a clubhouse. Federal authorities looked at Joe Conforte, the Mustang, the Old Bridge, the "Regas Drug Organization" and the Hells Angels and saw one, vast, ongoing criminal conspiracy. Local authorities saw that, too.

After the Renegades' intentions to become Hells Angels became public knowledge in June 1998, the Storey County Licensing Board served Burgess with an order to show cause why his brothel license should not be revoked. The board told Burgess to respond to complaints including but "not limited to" motorcycle noise, harassment of local residents and failure to pay his brothel license fee. But, virtually the entire hearing was about Burgess' association with the Angels. Board member Charles Haynes argued that the Angels were "known to be involved in organized crime, and anybody who does not realize that needs to wake up and come into the 20th century." Haynes and Storey County Sheriff Robert Del Carlo introduced into evidence articles about the Angels downloaded from the internet. Burgess argued that the Hells Angels did not meet at the Old Bridge and had no influence over it. Haynes responded, "If it looks like a duck and smells like a duck and it walks like a duck, it's a duck."

The Board revoked the license. Burgess filed an emergency petition to postpone the revocation in state court. The state court denied the petition. So Burgess filed a complaint in federal court arguing that the local Board had unconstitutionally deprived Burgess of his right of free association. The federal court prohibited the license revocation until a state appeals court reviewed the matter. Two years later the Nevada Supreme Court ruled that Burgess could continue to operate the Old Bridge even though he had joined the Hells Angels.

And, then there was still more drama.

In November 1999 an anti-prostitution crusader named Milo John Reese disappeared into the night after a meeting with Burgess at the Old Bridge Ranch. Reese, like Burgess and Joe Conforte before him, was part of the local color in Reno. He once proposed to open a gay brothel which,

64

he believed, would somehow expose the evils of legalized prostitution. Police found his car a half mile away from the Old Bridge the next morning. The car window had been broken with a rock and Reese's blood was found both inside and outside of the car. Suspicion immediately centered around Dave Burgess.

Another brothel owner named Dennis Hof, who would go on to appear numerous times on *HBO* starting in 2002, told reporters he didn't think Burgess had done anything to Reese. Hof who owned two legal brothels east of Carson City, defended Burgess and said he suspected Reese arranged his disappearance to get publicity. "I hope for his sake that he (Reese) is safe and secure someplace, but my guess is he will show up and they'll find David had nothing to do with it at all. My impression is that this is designed to hurt David. (Reese) has his opinions, but he's never done anything to irritate brothel owners because he's ineffective."

The search for Reese's body in the wild hills around the Old Bridge lasted almost a week before the anti-prostitution crusader was spotted on a surveillance camera at an automated teller machine in Sacramento. After Reese turned himself into police in Las Vegas he explained that he had pulled the stunt because he believed women from the Old Bridge were being sent to hotels in Reno where prostitution was illegal and he wanted to call attention to that. "It is very evident these girls at these brothels, all over Nevada, not just here, are doing a lot of business where prostitution is not legal," Reese said at a press conference. "I'm sorry I put everybody up to this, but I thought it was the only way to do it."

And, then there was even more drama and misfortune.

Sohn Regas was in Laughlin for the annual River Run biker rally in 2002. In the early morning of April 27, a long simmering dispute between Mongols Motorcycle Club members and Hells Angels erupted in a bar named Rosa's Cantina inside Harrah's Casino at one end of Laughlin's Casino Road. Three men, a Mongol named Anthony Salvador "Bronson" Barrera and two Hells Angels named Jeramie Dean Bell and Robert Emmet Tumelty were killed in the minute long mêlée. Sohn walked into Harrah's with Bell and Tumelty. He watched them die. Sohn is licensed to carry a firearm in Nevada but he was unarmed. After Bell and Tumelty were killed Sohn tackled a Mongol who was trying to hit him with a sign. Sohn was later charged with racketeering, nine counts of attempted murder and 12 counts of carrying a concealed weapon. Eventually, after a years-long legal ordeal, the charges were dismissed. The government's point was to use a complex racketeering prosecution as a way to punish Sohn and others for belonging to the Angels. Because of his prosperity, Burgess was able to help his brother in law and other Angels pay their legal bills.

*****

Three years and a day after the government seized the Mustang Ranch and its name, three months after the fight in Laughlin, Dave Burgess rechristened his whorehouse "The Mustang Ranch."

"I checked the copyright and patent laws and I found out that after three years a product or business name goes back into the public pool for reuse by the next bonafide user," Burgess explained. "A protected name can not be warehoused. The name has to be used in daily commerce to be protected. That means if the government wanted to protect the Mustang name, it needed to keep the brothel open."

"One day I got a visit from a federal agent telling me that they were going to take my Uncle Joe to trial for some crime even though he was still a federal fugitive. The agent then told me that I was going to be one of their main witnesses against my uncle. I told the agent he could go fuck himself. He then told me if I did not agree to be a co-operating witness for the government against Conforte, he would make sure that I would not be able to use the name Mustang Ranch. I just laughed at him and went about my business. By the way, during, or I should say, right after that visit, the agent knocked down my Mustang brothel sign with his pick-up truck and then drove away."

The "federal agent" was Kemp Shiffer, a senior criminal investigator for the IRS. Shiffer was behind most of the tax investigations into the Mustang Ranch. In 2003 Shiffer was "investigated" by Reno police after prostitutes alleged the tax agent used his IRS badge and the threat of criminal charges for tax evasion to coerce prostitutes into providing him with sex. Shiffer was never charged for that. But in 2011 Shiffer agreed to a plea deal that sentenced him to two years in prison, ten years of supervised release and 250 hours of community service after he was charged with multiple counts of pimping and of transporting a homeless 18 year old woman from California to Nevada and putting her to work as a whore.

A couple months after Shiffer threatened him Burgess "noticed that the government had put the Mustang Ranch building and the Mustang business name on the auction block on E-bay. It sold very quickly to my main competitor in the Reno area, about ten miles east of me." The competitor was Lance Gilman who bought the old Mustang buildings for $145,100 and moved them to his whorehouse, the Wild Horse Adult Resort and Spa. Gilman renovated the old buildings and used them as a second brothel which he called The Mustang Ranch. According to court documents in his charged case, Kemp Shiffer was a frequent visitor to Gilman's brothel where he did the taxes for most of the prostitutes.

Burgess won a temporary order that restrained Gilman from using the name. "The judge was so sure that the name legally belonged to me that he not only enjoined the other party from using the name, but he also let me continue to use the name Mustang Ranch for my business for about the next year or so while the case was progressing through the courts" Burgess said. There was a four day trial to decide the matter in December 2006 – seven months before the traffic stop in Wyoming.

"After that first day of trial," Burgess claims, "I stepped into the elevator to ride down, but before the door closed, a supposed unrelated third party stepped into the elevator with me and on the way down he told me I was wasting my time. The decision had already been made. And the decision was David Burgess loses."

"Well, I did lose that case and the Mustang Ranch business name. This time the judge stated that the government is so busy, it does not have to adhere to the federal laws that pertain to copyright issues. So I immediately re-filed the case with the Ninth Circuit Court of Appeals in San Francisco." The case was still under appeal when Burgess was arrested in Wyoming. His main concern after that arrest was that "a brothel license holder cannot be a convicted felon."

Burgess had been worried for years that he would be framed for something and then his brothel license would be revoked. That fear that he might be framed was one of the reasons why Burgess began the website *davesworld81*. The numeral following the title Dave's World is a common reference to the Hells Angels: Eight for the eighth letter of the alphabet, "H," and the numeral one for the first letter "A." The name had been suggested to Burgess by a Hells Angel named Dennis from Richmond, California.

Burgess just wanted the site to be a place where he could express his opinions. He was not particularly adept with or interested in computers. He didn't know any programming languages including Hypertext Markup Language, which is usually just shortened to HTML. But Dave's cousin Steven Byars, the disabled Vietnam vet, knew how to program a website. Burgess let him handle all the technical details. At first, "I would post things about my history in the legal brothel industry in the State of Nevada and post some things about public events that the club was sponsoring." Quickly, the focus of the site began to change.

While Byars kept the site up and running, Burgess concentrated on the content. *Davesworld81* became Burgess' blog, a home for his photographs, his thoughts and complaints about all the local, state and federal officials and agencies Dave thought were out to get him, and also a place for stories written by other Hells Angels who had things they wanted to say and no place to say them. The site included a page dedicated to his father, "Big Jim" Burgess. Mostly, the website reflected Burgess' resolution to live his life as openly as he could – thinking that would protect him from spurious accusations.

One of his first posts on the site read in full:

"Just in case you might be wondering why after all these years of being so private, I am now letting it all hang out with this website."

"Well after 20 years of having an illegal law enforcement wiretap on my home telephone, 19 years of having an illegal law enforcement wiretap on my business telephone, five years of having an illegal wiretap on my internet connection, three years of having an illegal law enforcement surveillance camera on the HAMC Nevada Nomads clubhouse in Reno/Sparks, unknown years of having an illegal surveillance camera on my home, I thought I would save all the taxpaying public some money by letting everyone see what's happening in Dave's World...for free."

"So enjoy your visit, I know the cops are enjoying theirs."

"And how do I know all this? Well about 21 years ago as the cops were leaving my apartment empty handed after serving me with one of the first 'secret witness' search warrants in the state of Nevada and then spending eight or so hours searching every square inch of my home, that cop and about ten of his buddies said, 'Mr. Burgess, this place is "too clean." We know you have someone on the inside.'"

Burgess relished the growing volume of his voice. Soon after the site went up, his front page said:

"A Note To All You Kids, And To Those Of You Who Act Like Kids – This Site May Contain Adult Stuff, So If You Are Not Old Enough to Make Informed Legal Decisions In Your Neighborhood, You Better Keep Out Or Santa Won't Visit You Next December. (Or better yet, go get your parents and let them help you make the decision on what parts of this website are cool for you.) Thanks From Your Pal Dave & And All His Little Helpers."

"To all the rest of you Motorcycle Enthusiasts, Warriors, Bikertrash, Headbangers, Journalists, Teachers, Citizens, Cops, Civil Servants, and the DOD, WELCOME TO THE WILD-WILD WEST."

Burgess was seduced by the idea that he was larger than life and too big to be framed. That was when he started calling himself "the Alpha Male." In some ways Burgess was foolish and reckless. For example, he never locked the doors to his home. Neighbors were free to come and go, open his refrigerator and use his swimming pool as they pleased. The Old Bridge Ranch's declared net income before taxes was about $2 million a year. Burgess appears to have given much of that away. For about two years before his arrest he seems to have convinced himself that he, rather than Dick Cheney, was in fact the Alpha Male – a photographer, writer, web publisher, Hells Angel, brothel owner and philanthropist who was irresistible to beautiful women. He lived with a drop dead gorgeous blonde named Misty. He loved flowers, an affection he acquired from Yvonne Regas who spent most of her life as a wholesale florist. He loved to garden. He hosted garden parties for what he called his "square neighbors," a very middle class couple named Joan and Wade Elam. And the Elams loved him. Almost everyone Burgess knew loved him. Except of course, for all his enemies.

One day a lobbyist from the Nevada Brothel Owners' Association visited Burgess' home. "He told me a story that

69

was told to him by the head of the FBI in Las Vegas. It was a warning to me to keep my doors locked because the government was setting the 'dirty tricks' guys loose on me. I was very naive. I thought no one in government would bother me as long as I wasn't breaking any laws. But after discussing the matter with the lobbyist, we decided that the government might try planting drugs around me to get the county to revoke my brothel license."

Another day, "A local defense attorney jogged by my house. I was working in my garden. He stopped and was jogging in place and he said, 'Hey David. I thought I would give you the heads-up. I am defending someone on a double murder case. The government wants to make some kind of deal with us if we are willing to implicate you in some way. My client assured them that he does not know you.' Then he jogged off."

In Burgess' mind, his government enemies started to grow. The year before his drug arrest, Burgess attended the Hells Angels National Run in Cody, Wyoming. That year, he said, "There was a relatively new law enforcement presence. They were none other than Homeland Security. Not just with their many midnight blue, blacked out Suburbans. They also had a midnight blue Black Hawk helicopter with the words 'Homeland Security' in silver on the sides. This helicopter would fly so close to our run site, a couple of times it almost blew over our huge run tents. Being the faithful photographer that I am, I climbed up onto the top of my motor home and I pointed my not so cheap camera at the helicopter and snapped a few shots." The photograph became the wallpaper for the homepage of *davesworld81*. "It was a full screen shot of that Black Hawk helicopter with some agent hanging out of the door of the helicopter taking my picture. I am sure my photo of him was at least as good as his photo of me. I'll bet he didn't post the picture of me on his homepage. And, I am also sure every biker taskforce agent on the planet had access to that photograph of me. With the picture I also posted the price of the helicopter, the number of personal it took to man the helicopter, their daily wages plus the hazard pay they would receive, plus the price of fuel, the hotel cost, the tarmac fees at the local airport, and I can't remember what else. I captioned the photo, 'Taxpayers of America, what else is our government wasting your hard earned tax dollars on?'"

Burgess was convinced that the traffic stop and search in Wyoming on the way to the National Run in 2007 was part of an ongoing plot to put the last remnant of the original Mustang Ranch out of business. He thought defending himself against the drug charges would be expensive and he knew his ownership of the brothel was in real jeopardy but he hardly panicked. He had been close to and personally gone through so many legal dramas that he expected to persevere, somehow. His drug trial was scheduled to begin on December 3rd. It was a small case. The search that found the drugs was probably illegal. The total amount of drugs was less than two ounces.

Then the FBI Swat burst into his home and he found out that he was in much greater peril than he could have imagined.

The Case

The legal case against Dave Burgess was dramatically compelling.

The case was that he was an immoral man – a whoremonger whose closest friends were all members of a powerful cabal of dangerous and depraved gangsters who called themselves Hells Angels. He was, the prosecution would try to prove, a cynical psychopath and a kind of computer genius – as psychopaths are often geniuses – who was so accomplished with computers that he actually had a website. Jaded, after years of exploiting vulnerable and innocent whores for profit, Burgess could only satisfy his vile appetites by masturbating over images of suffering children. His addiction to this vice was so advanced that he obsessively amassed the largest collection of child pornography ever discovered. And, he was so consumed that he took his vast and meticulously organized library of child pornography with him on his Hells Angels vacation. He was so obsessed that he even brought a backup of his child pornography collection with him, possibly to share with his fellow degenerates. His vice so controlled his life that he had actually exploited a child in his care, immortalized that exploitation with obscenely captioned photographs and brought those along with him to share with other Hells Angel degenerates at their satanic gathering in the wilds of Arkansas – possibly as they all danced naked in the moonlight around a great, flaming pentagram, chanting "All hail Hell! All hail Hell!" Simultaneously, like a serial killer in a movie – like the character Paul White in the 1988 thriller *White of the Eye* – the brilliant, evil and obsessed Burgess managed to hide his true self from all the men and women closest to him.

The judge and prosecutor thought these presumptions rang true. Unfortunately, so did Dave Burgess' defense attorney.

But, tempting as it might be for right thinking Americans – good people like all you good, admirable, hardworking folks now reading these words; tempted though you should be – to see the truth in these often tacit

72

presumptions there is another, remotely possible, explanation for the damning evidence used to indict Dave Burgess. And that is, Dave Burgess was framed.

Unlikely as it seemed to all the officers of the federal court in Cheyenne, Wyoming, in order to cover all the bases in the case one must allow that there is a possibility that Dave Burgess was guilty of none of this and that all of the evidence that would be used against him at trial had been manufactured and planted: To punish Dave Burgess for being who he was, to possibly convince Burgess to betray his friends, to embarrass the Hells Angels and to strip Burgess of the last of his Aunt Sally and Uncle Joe's Mustang Ranch.

The judge, prosecutor and defender in the case thought the possibility that Dave Burgess had been framed was so far fetched that all three refused to consider it or even allow it to be mentioned.

*****

After the Freightliner was towed into Evanston, before Russ Schmitt wrote Trooper Arnell's affidavit in support of a search warrant, Schmitt called Elvin Ehrhardt in Cheyenne. Ehrhardt was a Senior Investigator with the Wyoming Division of Criminal Investigation's Intelligence Unit. In his own words, Ehrhardt collected "intelligence on criminal organizations and individuals involving, uh, well, involving gang type of activity. And that covers a lot of different aspects: Street gangs, prison gangs, motorcycle groups."

Wyoming doesn't have a problem with gangs but the Division of Criminal Investigation's interest in "gangs" does illustrate the metamorphosis of America's various local and state police forces into components of what is, in effect, a single federal police department that shares "intelligence" through something called the National Criminal Intelligence Sharing Plan. The information is also shared with at least 67 "Fusion Centers." Most of this national spy apparatus is funded as part of the Global War on Terror. The Departments of Justice and Homeland Security both consider the Hells Angels to be a "transnational drug gang" that threatens the security of the nation, which is why the pack of Angels was surveilled from the time they left Reno. Ehrhardt was gathering intelligence for the federal government – which the federal government would share with every other police department in the United States, Canada, Western Europe and Australia – and although he was, technically, an employee of Wyoming the money for Ehrhardt's job was federal money. He was probably expecting to hear that someone had nabbed Dave Burgess. Every other cop in Wyoming was on the lookout for the "War Wagon." And he almost betrayed that anticipation in testimony. "I received a call that we had..." he began to say. Then using the anacolunthonic syntax typical of testifying cops he continued, "...of the contact with Mr. Burgess' vehicle."

Ehrhardt was present for the search. And, at its conclusion Ehrhardt began a record of the official chain of custody of the only items found in the Freightliner that were not marijuana or cocaine. According to Ehrhardt's notes he took possession of the laptop and two portable hard drives at 8:30 p.m. on July 24th and he locked them in "Intelligence Safe number two" at DCI headquarters in Cheyenne five hours later. He was so concerned about the items that he reopened the safe at nine the next morning and made a note, "Checked items. Still secure. Was planning to transfer items to ICAC for analysis, however ICAC out. Locked back in Intel safe number two 09:30 hours. Will transfer on 7/26." No one ever wondered why he would write such a strange memo to himself except to falsify the chain of custody of the evidence. Maybe when he went home that night, Ehrhardt opened his refrigerator and wrote himself another note. "Refrigerator light still works at 6:26 p.m. Was worried light might be about to burn out. Will check again tomorrow." Ehrhardt also testified multiple times under oath that he never tried to "access, tamper with, or in any way alter the digital material" contained on the hardware.

ICAC is an acronym for Internet Crimes Against Children. There are 61, federally funded ICAC Task Forces in the United States including the one in Cheyenne which is part of the Wyoming Department of Criminal Investigation. At the time of Burgess' arrest, the Cheyenne ICAC Task Force was headed by a man named Flint Waters. When Burgess was arrested, ICAC was staffed by five DCI agents, one Homeland Security agent and one FBI agent.

Ehrhardt transferred custody of the hardware to DCI Special Agent Randall Huff. Huff, a rosy faced man with a thin mustache who bears an unfortunate resemblance to the 1950s character actor Broderick Crawford, is a computer forensics

74

expert within Cheyenne ICAC. It would be logical to expect him to conduct the search for evidence of Dave Burgess' drug dealing – for trophy photos and pay-owe slips and all the specious evidence Russ Schmitt told a country judge must be there – but Agent Huff, the official story goes, simply held onto the hardware for a week. No one bothered to ask Huff if he had ever accessed, tampered with or in any way altered the digital material.

Then Huff transferred official custody of the hardware to DCI Special Agent Scott Hughes. Hughes job at ICAC also is to forensically verify the existence of child pornography on computers and when he got the hardware attributed to Burgess it was unaccompanied by any paperwork. There was absolutely nothing to connect the hardware to Dave Burgess except blind faith. So, Hughes has testified, he requested a copy of the original search warrant from Russ Schmitt. For some reason – and like everything else in the Burgess case there are multiple, evolving explanations – the warrant did not arrive in Cheyenne until August 21 and by then that search warrant had expired and there was no longer any legal basis for a search.

So Hughes went upstairs to meet with David L. Delicath, the Senior Assistant Attorney General of the State of Wyoming. No record of the meeting exists although the official story is that the two men talked about the implications of the expired warrant. Then nothing happened for another week. But finally, on September 6th, a paralegal named Deborah Cordova who worked in Delacath's office told Hughes to go ahead and search the computer anyway, "but to stop searching and obtain a new search warrant if he found any non-drug related contraband on the computer." The paralegal gave Hughes permission to search the computer – the paralegal – as if Delicath understood the toxicity and danger of what was going on and needed to cover his ass with a clean, white diaper of plausible deniability. The warning to get a new "warrant if he found any non-drug related contraband on the computer" also seems particularly contrived. Exactly what kind of "contraband" did the paralegal think that might be? Plans for the atomic bomb? A list of American secret agents? Bootlegged movies?

The first step in computer searches is to make an exact copy of the suspect hard drive. Hughes used a piece of software called EnCase to accomplish that. Creating a copy of a drive can sometimes take more than a dozen hours but

EnCase has a preview function which shows examiners what is being copied. Hughes did not begin his search with the laptop. He started instead with the Maxtor portable hard drive – the drive that Burgess maintains he left at home but that Trooper Arnell found hidden under a couch – in a niche so tight that Arnell had to remove his watch in order to retrieve it. That Maxtor drive, just like the one Burgess had left in a drawer, was broken and was unaccompanied by any other hardware like a USB or FireWire cord. Hughes had to disassemble the drive and use one of his cords in order to connect it to his computer.

In the official court record: "…on September 6, 2007, (Hughes) began the process of acquiring (or copying) and previewing the contents of the Maxtor External Hard Drive. The EnCase preview function utilized by Special Agent Hughes permitted him to view images while the process of acquiring the contents of the hard drive proceeded. This preview revealed 'multiple images of child exploitation.' Special Agent Hughes testified he noted the name of the file, minimized the image, allowed the acquisition process to continue, but immediately stopped looking at images. Thereafter, a search warrant was applied for and obtained in Laramie County, Wyoming, which authorized the search of the laptop and the two external hard drives. Following execution of the search warrants specific to the laptop and external hard drives, further evidence of child exploitation was found and the instant charges were brought against defendant Burgess."

Hughes stopped counting the perverted pictures after he reached 1,300 but he would later state that of the 166,000 images (or page views) on the Maxtor hard drive, at least 35% were child pornography – which amounts to about 58,000 images. It was an unprecedented amount of pornography. Nicole Balliett, the Homeland Security Agent in the Cheyenne ICAC Task Force, would testify at an evidentiary hearing a year later, on November 4, 2008, on the amount of child pornography stored in her office. She was questioned by the federal prosecutor who tried Burgess, James Anderson

Q. And so you folks maintain – as part of the ICAC team mission – you folks maintain a library or catalog of images of child pornography?

A. Yes we do.

Q How big is that catalog?

A It is over 50,000 images.

Q. Over 50,000 images?

A .Yes

Q. And those take up not only still images, but movies; is that: correct?

A. Correct.

The Homeland Security Agent's testimony is interesting because the Maxtor portable hard drive, putatively found under a couch in Burgess' Freightliner was widely reported to contain to contain 70,000 pornographic images of children – a number a little more dramatic than Agent Hughes estimate.

Most troubling for Burgess, however, was who was in some of those images. David and his live in girlfriend had taken in the young daughter of one of his club brothers, a man named Tracy Lee Curtis. The then 14 year old girl was named Rachael Curtis. She had been abandoned by her mother and when her father was temporarily unable to care for her Burgess assumed that responsibility. It was his duty as a Hells Angel, and particularly as the president of his charter, to ensure that the girl was well brought up. And as far as anyone could tell, she was. She was a pretty, rambunctious dark haired girl and some of the photos found on both hard drives were nude or semi-nude photos of her. Worst of all, the photos had been lewdly captioned by a sexual pervert.

One photo showed Rachael taking a shower with a superimposed caption that read, "I think this is one of the sexiest pictures in my collection. Rachael I caught naked in the motel room shower with her belly all pushing out and her oh so erect nipples! I think I'll jack off now." Rachael was photographed again, sitting cross legged on a bed wearing only a towel with her genitals exposed. That photo was captioned, "Uncle David's pussy meat princess." There were several photos of the girl's soiled panties. One of those photos had the long caption, "Friday, May 25, 2007, @12:45 p.m. we get a motel room in Winnemucca. Rachael says she wants to take a shower so I leave the room. When I get back her dirty under panties on the floor outside the bathroom, so I picked them up and saw the fresh creamy little stain she left for me. So I sniffed 'em for a second and took a picture of them, and then I sucked her fresh pussy-goo out of the crotch." Another doctored photo showed Rachael's head on the body of woman engaged in the physical act of love. Another caption claimed there were "still more than a few naughty little secrets that only she and I know about." Yet another photo was captioned "I even let Uncle David take some of his pervert pictures between my legs again." Another caption read, "My Uncle David is taking pictures, of me and I have a dirty pussy infection."

The glaring change in prose voice in the captions, alternating between the point of view of a stereotypical pedophile and the point of view of his vulnerable victim suggested that Burgess might actually be mentally ill. The references to "Uncle David," also contained a stereotypical innuendo about trusted family members who molest their relatives. It was in fact, how the children of Hells Angels often address their fathers' club brothers. It was all enormously embarrassing for the Hells Angels Motorcycle Club. In the coming months the phrases "Hells Angels" and "child porn" would be repeatedly linked in newspaper headlines. Most Hells Angels were outraged that one of their own had allowed himself to be accused of such crimes. Fearsome and well-known members of the club publically stated their wish that Burgess would get what was "coming to him."

There was no limit to the unspeakable horrors stored on the Maxtor portable drive. To even briefly allude to all of Dave Burgess' alleged obsessions is to flog the reader and make him want to look away. The Maxtor held two dozen images of infants, under the age of one, being sexually violated. All of the obscenity was obsessively catalogued. There were, the police said, 23 pages of file directories with titles like "blonde, butts, camel toe, between legs, new slideshow, wedgy, animated gif, animals, cunt, head, miscellaneous, backyards, nastiest 1yo series, sausage play" and "sausage in the ass."

The ICAC investigators never revealed how many of these images were new to them. If the Burgess bust yielded 70,000 images and ICAC had previously only known about and catalogued 50,000 images, logic would seem to dictate that the Maxtor hard drive was a landmark in the fight against child sexual exploitation. It might also have been worth some effort to discover, with the exception of the two dozen or so photos of Rachael Curtis, how all this filth came to be on the Maxtor and how duplicates of much of it arrived on the Seagate portable hard drive that Burgess had acknowledged taking with him on his vacation and had left sitting out during Arnell's traffic stop.

But investigation wasn't what the Cheyenne ICAC Task Force did. The organization was first of all a highly effective punishment machine. The Task Force epitomized what Andrew Carlon, writing in the *Virginia Law Review*, called "the sadistic state…a totalitarian punishment machine…which wields power, most fully realized through the infliction of pain, as an end in itself, the human beings in its power merely means to that awful end" and "raises the specter of totalitarianism…marked by, among other things, the replacement of the suspected offense by the possible crime."

At the time of Burgess' arrest, Cheyenne ICAC identified about 1600 cases of possession of child pornography a year, Typically the team would prosecute two cases a week. Most of those cases were resolved with plea bargains. About 25 cases each year would go to trial in a federal courtroom in Cheyenne. From 2005 on, Cheyenne ICAC had a 100 percent conviction rate, which immediately invites the question: What do you suppose the conviction rate is in North Korea? Cheyenne ICAC was and remains a federally funded program so Cheyenne's long reach identified kiddie porn owners nationwide, from Florida to San Diego. Some potential pedophiles were enticed and trapped in the sorts of stings made famous on the former *NBC* "news" show *To Catch a Predator.* An ICAC Agent, for example Agent Balliett, would entice a dimwit to Cheyenne with the promise of sex with a virgin and when the dimwit arrived he would be arrested.

But Cheyenne ICAC was also a software developer. The man in charge of Cheyenne ICAC, Flint Waters, was a software professional. In 2004 Waters, his colleague Special Agent Robert Leazenby of the Wyoming Division of Criminal Investigation and Bill Wiltse of the Salem, Oregon Police Department developed a software program that identified and tracked computers that traded child pornography. That was what the 50,000 images in the Cheyenne ICAC library were about. Water's software looked for those images on the internet 24 hours a day seven days a week. If Burgess had acquired his vast library as every other pedophilia voyeur had, one of the dozens of ICAC task forces in the United States would have caught him at it.

The internet is where most of child porn voyeurs find their images. As recently as 1975 and the publication of *Show Me!: A Picture Book of Sex for Children and Parents* by St. Martin's Press, no one tried to police child pornography. Most men who wanted child pornography bought it in book stores that sold other kinds of pornography. But virtually all rational

Americans understand that child pornography, as zealots state over and over, are images of actual crimes. The first federal law prohibiting the manufacture and commercial distribution of child porn was passed in 1978 and then amended in 1984 in an attempt to differentiate child porn from other forms of pornography that the Supreme Court had ruled were legal. By the middle of Ronald Reagan's first term the stores that sold child porn were hounded out of existence and the social problem of child pornography seemed to have been solved. But then virtually everyone in the world became connected to the internet and child pornography began to be traded electronically.

The first federal investigation of child pornography distributed on the internet was in 1993 and the first case of possessing child pornography on a computer wasn't brought until May 1995 – against a man named David Rey Luera in Los Angeles. Luera was fined $1,350, sentenced to three years of probation and 240 hours of community service, ordered to register as a sex offender and ordered to forfeit his home computer. Luera was arrested three years later for downloading child pornography and was again sentenced to three years probation. The war on child porn on the internet began to heat up in 1997 when it suddenly appeared that there were fantasy pedophiles everywhere. Larry Matthews, an editor for *National Public Radio* who was researching a story about pedophilia, was arrested for transmitting and receiving child pornography over the Internet. The next year a Yale professor named Antonio C. Lasaga was arrested by the FBI for downloading child porn. The year after that, Michael Blutrich, a potential witness against John Gotti, was dropped from the witness list after he downloaded child porn. Suddenly child pornography seemed to be everywhere but it wasn't. What happened was that police found out that child pornography both outraged most citizens and was an easy crime to prosecute – because virtually all offenders are caught red handed. There is always a synergy between outrage and prosecution and outraging Wyoming and the rest of the nation was another thing Wyoming ICAC did well. Flint Waters, a doughy, dour, balding man with an impressive mustache, became a Wyoming celebrity.

Although only about 2,000 child pornography cases were prosecuted in America the year Burgess was arrested, Waters said over and over that that there were "hundreds" of child porn collections in Wyoming alone. He invented the fact that "300,000 to 500,000 computers" trade images of child exploitation and he found "600,000 computers" that contained "illegal pornography." He described regular interviews with the men he prosecuted. "They'll look you in the eye. They'll describe it. They'll get excited about their interest. They'll talk about how society just hasn't caught up and this is what they should be doing. I've arrested them, have them get out on bond and on the way home pick up another computer and get back online to find the material." Waters found that like the Terminator, child pornography enthusiasts just "don't stop."

Waters frequently and publically bragged about the men he had brought to ruin. His two most memorable seemed to be "a Master Chief in the United States Air Force in charge of security forces at Warren Air Force Base" and "a 42-year-old web site developer from Colorado Springs."

Waters told the U.S. Senate, "We are also seeing modifications of these movies and images. Offenders are compiling the material in online instruction manuals, training each other how to rape children in ways that make it more difficult to detect, in ways that are harder to prove during medical examinations." Really?

Waters became the chief training officer for 46 ICAC Teams around the country. He trained cops in 17 countries in techniques to make child porn cases. He "accompanied and acted as an advisor to Laura Bush" when she travelled to Paris to attend "an international conference addressing the global problem of online child exploitation."

Oprah Winfrey described him as "a father of four" who "has devoted his life to patrolling the Internet to take down child predators."

Waters told Oprah how difficult on him his crusade to protect children had been. "I don't mean it to sound like it's hard for law enforcement – its gut wrenching" Waters said. "But those kids who are waiting for us – that's who it's hard for. That's who we need to be able to try and reach out to." He explained that America couldn't eradicate the scourge of child sexual exploitation until the nation got serious and threw some real money at the problem. "We're getting better at finding them, seeing who's out there," he told America's most influential billionaire. "We're just overwhelmed by the numbers."

Waters appeared on Winfrey's television show to urge all right thinking Americans to support the passage of the

81

"PROTECT Our Children Act," which would "provide valuable funding for child protection task forces." Like his. Winfrey told viewers that supporting the bill was something they could do if they were "enraged, disgusted and fed up with child predators slipping through the cracks."

The bill, which was sponsored by Joe Biden and became law in 2009, provided about $1 billion "to improve the Internet Crimes Against Children Task Force, to increase resources for regional computer forensic labs, and to make other improvements to increase the ability of law enforcement agencies to investigate and prosecute child predators." Apparently it was a good start but not quite good enough. In 2009 Cheyenne ICAC received a grant funded by the American Recovery and Reinvestment Act, a law intended "to preserve and create jobs and promote economic recovery; to assist those most impacted by the recession," in the amount of $424,573. The money was used "to pay the salary, overtime, training, travel, vehicle, investigative and equipment costs" for one additional investigator.

The crimes discovered and substantiated by Cheyenne ICAC were most often prosecuted by Assistant United States Attorney James C. Anderson – a man with a Harley, a prospector's beard and a mean streak – the man who interrogated Homeland Security Agent Nicole Balliett and who prosecuted Dave Burgess. Anderson has spent virtually his entire career as a prosecutor and his specialty was ensuring that Cheyenne ICAC kept its unblemished conviction rate. He also served as an instructor at the Wyoming Law Enforcement Academy and at various ICAC conferences around the country.

In late June 2007, Anderson told *The Associated Press* that Wyoming, with a population of about 535,000 was "pursuing 720 child pornography investigations" within the state. And, it is reasonable to say that Anderson would have liked to put all 720 of those suspects in prison and throw away the key.

In an article in the August 2007 edition of *Wyoming Lawyer*, Anderson did his part to sound the alarm that virtually every toddler was in danger of being raped by someone her parents had been foolish enough to trust. Anderson informed his readers. "In calendar year 2000, a total of six online exploitation of children cases were filed in the Wyoming U.S. District Court. In 2007, as of July 1st, 23 cases have been filed." And he conflated the Congressional testimony of a witness named Dr. Sharon Cooper, a professional expert witness in the field of forensic pediatrics – possibly the only forensics pediatrics expert witness in the world – with "recent studies which indicate that those who regularly view child pornography are more likely to sexually abuse children. Additionally, as the Internet and related technologies have grown, children have become increasingly at risk of being sexually solicited online by predators."

Like any salesman, Anderson told his audience they had a serious problem and if they agreed to buy what he was selling their serious problem could be solved. "One in five youth Internet users received an unwanted sexual solicitation within the past year," Anderson warned. "Wyoming has responded to this problem." And then he lauded Flint Waters and his little band of heroes at Cheyenne ICAC. In the popular imagination, prosecutors are men who care about justice. In reality, prosecutors are men who care about convictions.

In case after case in Cheyenne, Anderson acted as an advocate for ICAC. He had a polished folksiness in court and a small bag of tricks that his experience had shown guaranteed convictions. In fairness to Anderson, he may simply be stupid. He genuinely seems to believe that the discovery of child pornography on a computer proves the owner put it there. In a trial in January 2008, of a man who insisted he never looked at child pornography or stored it on his computer, Anderson told a jury:

"…In fact, when they first did an onsite preview of the defendant's machine at his house, the software that they were using didn't show any child pornography and, as a result of that, they gave him a break. They said, "Well, gee, we will just take the hard drive for a couple of days and examine it, but if we do find pornography, then things will be different."

In that trial Anderson asked Randall Huff, the same agent who took possession of Burgess' computer equipment for a week but never looked at it: "Is that…when you folks do a forensic exam of a computer, do you ever really get finished?"

"No,' Huff replied. "You can go on with these forever. It is like trying to find the end of the Internet. There's just so much information in these forensics that we can continue to dig and dig and dig."

"And one of the reasons, there's just huge, massive amounts of storage or information to be stored on a hard drive, right?"

"Correct."

What neither Anderson nor Huff explained was that child pornography, malware, and other malicious information may be stored in areas of a hard drive that are inaccessible by a computer owner using his operating system and can only be discovered using drive mapping and duplication programs like EnCase.

Those cases, though comparatively rare, illustrate an important concept in American law: The idea of "guilty mind" or, in lawyer's Latin, *mens rea*. In order to be guilty of a crime, one must be aware that one has performed the action that results in a crime. The absence of a guilty mind is the foundation of the insanity defense.

A growing number of personal computers throughout the world are now compromised with malware that transforms those computers into "zombies" and as a result the *mens rea* defense has begun to appear in child pornography cases. Typically in those cases, child pornography is downloaded to computers without the owner's knowledge or permission. The child porn is not accessible to the owner but a "zombie operator" can both access and share the pornography stored on the zombie computer. When one of the many ICAC Task Forces discovers the illegal content, the defendant must hire a computer forensics technician to tell the jury how the illicit photos got there without the defendant's knowledge or cooperation.

By the time Burgess was arrested, Anderson had become so used to putting people in jail for possession of child pornography that he had his own cynical vocabulary for innocent defendants and their defense experts.

"And what's the defense," Anderson asked in that January 2008 trial, " Ladies and gentlemen of the jury, I will tell you what the defense is. We even have an acronym for this defense. If you talk to any cop or any prosecutor they will know what this acronym means – S-O-D-D-I. SODDI. You know what that stands for? Some Other Dude Did It. Some Other Dude Did It. And we see it all the time in courts. And ladies and gentlemen, please, when you're considering this defense, think about the credibility of the witnesses that have appeared before you. Please think about the credibility of the witnesses before you, and in making your assessment of credibility carefully scrutinize all of the testimony given by a witness."

Then, in the same trial, to disparage the defendant's forensic experts who had testified there was no proof that the defendant had loaded pornography on his computer, Anderson continued, "And consider – consider the relation a witness may bear to either side of the case. And, you know what, what was the – what was the relation of the paid witness? Well, you know, if you're charging $250 an hour, you better deliver a product. You better deliver a product." As opposed to the idealists who worked for Flint Waters.

"Then we have the paid witness, Tami Loehrs," Anderson continued. "Charges $250 an hour, and she doesn't seem to know the role between an expert and an advocate. You know what? Somebody that comes in a courtroom as an expert owes a jury, owes the Court some objectivity. Some objectivity. You're not supposed to be coloring your answers and only doing their work selectively. Instead she comes in and she wants to talk about anomalies and talk in generalizations and so on. And you know what, ladies and gentlemen, if you think carefully about her testimony, all she offers you is speculation. All she offers you is conjecture. And it is twisted into making it sound like it is authoritative and the real deal. But it isn't. It isn't."

*****

Anderson fought Dave Burgess' case tooth and nail. On November 13th, Anderson filed a motion to deny Burgess bail on the grounds that he was charged with a "crime of violence;" there was a "serious risk defendant will flee;" that because he was a Hells Angel there was a "serious risk of obstruction of justice;" that he was a risk to other people "and the community;" and that he was probably guilty of a "ten year drug offense."

Burgess made his initial court appearance in Reno federal court on November 16th before a federal judge named Robert McQuaid. He convinced McQuaid that his finances had been frozen by the Internal Revenue Service and the judge ordered that a federal public defender be appointed for him. Burgess was ordered to appear at the U.S. Marshall's Office in Cheyenne on November 26th for an arraignment hearing that afternoon. He was released on "home incarceration" without bail and appeared, as he had promised, in Cheyenne before Magistrate William C. Beaman. That's where he met both Anderson and his own public defender, a man named Jim Barrett.

James H. Barrett's most attractive personal quality was his name. He was the grandson of a four-term Congressman, Governor and United States Senator named Frank A. Barrett. His father, Dr. Francis Barrett, was the Governor's oldest son and he was named for his uncle, Judge James E. Barrett who served as Wyoming's attorney general before his appointment to the Tenth U.S. Circuit Court of Appeals.

At their first meeting Barrett and Anderson both urged Burgess to take a plea deal. Barrett thought going to trial would be "an inconvenience." Burgess and everyone he knew insisted he had been framed by someone and they naively expected that Barrett would put some effort into trying to find out who. Troy Regas, who had deeply distrusted federal justice ever since he was framed, his father was framed and his mother was indicted, told Barrett that Burgess had been framed. "Regas suggested Barrett and (his private investigator Steve) Brinkerhoff look into (1) an apparently psychotic former brothel employee who had broken into Burgess' home and had been posting on-line statements accusing Burgess of operating a child pornography ring, (2) Lance Gillman, a business rival who had obtained the right to use the name Mustang Ranch, (3) Joe Conforte, a fugitive and Burgess' uncle with a long-standing conflict regarding the family brothel business, and (4) a recently-released-from prison ex-boyfriend of Burgess' former long-term girlfriend, Misty Beckman."

Barrett listened politely. Dave Burgess was the tenth federal child pornography case Barrett had defended in the last five years and he hadn't won a child porn case yet. Anderson told the magistrate that Burgess' computer drives were "chock full" of child porn, that Burgess was a Hells Angel, a flight risk and the owner of a whore house. "It's a legal occupation," Anderson said. "But I would characterize it as an unsavory occupation." Anderson also complained that Burgess should not be represented by a public defender. He told Beaman, "It looks to me like the defendant's got a net worth of several million dollars."

Beaman told Anderson to file a petition and ordered that Burgess be allowed to fly back home: "continue bond as set in Nevada and additional conditions are no access to computers, internet except on computer currently in home, submit to searches of his home computer, no unsupervised contact with anyone under 18 yrs, engage in substance abuse evaluation/treatment if directed by Pretrial Services, not to use software to erase or destroy internet history, turn over electronic storage media he is in possession of and not obtain any new media, access to internet restricted as to pornographic material (child pornography or otherwise), wireless access to computer not allowed, only allowed to be on internet to write his articles on his web site, no research, no google." And, "no unsupervised contact with any person under the ages of 18 years."

Burgess later said that Anderson offered him a deal that day "but part of the deal was that I would lose my brothel. Not sell it. Just close it and lose it. Again, I said no deal." Why Anderson would care about the Old Bridge Ranch is another element of the case that has never been explained.

Burgess' "home incarceration," was intended to approximate prison. Burgess was to remain a prisoner in his home at all times except for preapproved medical appointments or court appearances and his telephone use was limited. He thought that it was important that he be assigned to less restrictive "home detention" which would allow him to leave the house to work on his case. Barrett told Burgess he would work on that but he did not – not for months.

The case was assigned to Judge Alan Johnson. The then 69-year-old Alan Bond Johnson had been a judge since 1971. He was appointed a federal district judge by Ronald Reagan in 1985. He is a round, pink, bald man. His official portrait, painted by the esteemed artist Michele Rushworth, was hung with some ceremony in the Cheyenne federal courthouse in 2012. Johnson set a trial date of February 4th, 2008.

The day after Christmas, Anderson filed his motion to strip Burgess of his public defender.

Barrett seemed overwhelmed from the start. The first motion he filed in the case, on December 20th, was a continuance to file additional motions. On January 3rd, Barrett filed a second motion to continue further motions citing: "…counsel for the Defendant would advise the Court that work on dispositive motions in this matter have been delayed due to holidays, but primarily due to the illness and death of a close personal friend of counsel for the Defendant which has significantly delayed counsel's ability to complete the draft and research prior to the filing of Defendant's motions." That continuance was also granted.

Barrett filed a motion to suppress the evidence seized from the Freightliner on January 14th on the grounds that the search was unconstitutional. On January 29th, he filed a motion requesting a continuance of the trial in part because there was still no ruling by Judge Johnson on either the suppression issue or on whether Burgess would be allowed a public defender. Barrett also told the judge: "Additionally, it has come to the attention of the Defendant and has been confirmed by the government that a search warrant issued in the State and District of Nevada authorizing the search of the Defendant's home and business may also have resulted in the seizure of materials relevant to the present prosecution. Furthermore, Defendant has been advised by counsel for the government that it may be necessary to travel to the District of Nevada for the purpose of reviewing the materials seized from the Defendant's residence and business."

Barrett never reviewed the evidence discovered in the FBI search until trial was already underway. Anderson still hadn't filed a response to Barrett's motion to suppress on January 31st. Johnson gave him until February 12th to file his objection and on the same day the judge reset the trial for March 31st.

Johnson reviewed Burgess' finances and allowed him a public defender on February 1st and scheduled a hearing on suppression of the search for March 3rd. On March 5th, in response to a request filed by Anderson, Johnson continued the trial until April 14th.

Barrett went on vacation on March 22nd and refused to talk to Burgess while he was gone. He was feeling pressured. He was totally unprepared for Burgess' trial and he had another trial scheduled to begin on April 21st. He would have to prepare for that after Dave Burgess' trial was underway. When Barrett went back to work, a week before Dave's trial, he finally filed a motion requesting that his client's home incarceration be modified to home detention. Judge Johnson granted the modification the next day. Five days before trial, on April 9th, Johnson finally denied Barrett's motion to suppress. As far as Johnson was concerned, the two searches of the Freightliner were perfectly constitutional. The final pretrial hearing was on Friday, April 11th. The trial was scheduled to begin the following Monday.

*****

Barrett had not hired an independent computer forensics expert to look at the material on the incriminating hard drives. Because of the provisions of the then new Adam Walsh Child Protection and Safety Act of 2006, the hard drives could not be removed from the ICAC offices in Cheyenne. Any forensic work had to be done there under the supervision of an ICAC agent. By his own account Barrett had "looked at" the hard drives and the images they contained three times. His investigator, Steve Brinkerhoff , had made six trips to the ICAC offices to stare at the kiddie porn. The two men stared as the stupid monkeys stared at the black monolith in *2001 A Space Odyssey* – without either insight or inspiration. They confirmed that the images were disgusting and illegal. They confirmed that the text superimposed over the photos of Rachael Curtis was depraved. It never occurred to either man that there might be ways to find out how the images had arrived on the Maxtor and Seagate drives.

Burgess and Barrett had hardly talked since the arraignment. They did have a conversation when Burgess flew to Cheyenne for the March 3rd hearing but Barrett refused to return his client's calls. In the five months after the arraignment, Barrett's paralegal had sent Burgess copies of just one of the court filings in his case. And Burgess felt particularly trapped by the conditions of his home incarceration. Barrett had told Burgess that he had "dropped the ball" on that. Finally, the week before his trial was scheduled to start, when he was allowed to leave his home, Burgess started looking for a new lawyer and the money to pay him.

In two days Burgess found an experienced attorney named David Chesnoff who agreed to represent him and Burgess raised $45,000 to start paying him. Since Chesnoff was not a member of the Wyoming Bar, Burgess arranged for the slickest criminal lawyer in Cheyenne, Dion Custis, to act as counsel of record while Chesnoff sought permission to act as Burgess' attorney in Wyoming *pro hac vice* – which is Latin for "just this once." But since Burgess hadn't hired Chesnoff until Thursday and his trial started Monday, he needed Judge

Johnson to postpone the trial for at least two weeks and probably a month. That April 11th hearing epitomized the case.

The hearing was scheduled for 3:30 Friday afternoon and Barrett was late. In his place was a young public defender named Daniel Blythe, whom Burgess had never seen before. The court called Barrett on his cell phone. While the clerk placed the call Blythe told Judge Johnson that Custis, "has indicated an intention or has a suggestion or interest in entering an appearance in this case, and I have his cell phone, if at some point you choose to call him, too."

The judge sneered, "I assume if he had a sincere interest he would be here."

And Blythe tried to explain, "Well, he has a sincere interest, but he was…he's on his way or is in Denver at this time."

Then, on a speaker in the courtroom, Barrett said, "Hello."

"Jim?"

"I'm sorry, Judge."

"Are you still sitting in Judge Downes' courtroom?"

"No, I'm now sitting behind the wheel about 20 miles from Cheyenne. Twenty or 30."

"We'll wait for you."

"All right, Judge."

"We'll stand in recess."

When he arrived in the courtroom forty minutes later Barrett explained to Johnson that Burgess wanted another lawyer. "In a nutshell, Mr. Burgess wants to fire our office. He's unhappy. He's lost confidence. We're railroading him. We're doing any number of terrible things, neglecting him, haven't kept him fully advised. He hasn't seen all the discovery. He hasn't been taken to ICAC, and other, other and various failings and deficiencies on our part that have been communicated to him, I understand. Although I haven't heard it from Mr. Burgess or these other lawyers, by other attorneys." Which was mostly because Barrett had spent the entire case ignoring Burgess. That hearing was the third time Burgess saw the man who would defend him and it was only the third time the two had talked.

Johnson wanted to know, "Do you consider yourself ready to proceed?"

"I do," Barrett said. "You know, it's…let's put it this way. If Mr. Burgess…I don't want to force Mr. Burgess to a trial with anybody he doesn't have confidence in. I don't want to force Mr. Burgess to a trial with anybody he can't communicate with. I want Mr. Burgess to feel comfortable and to feel that he has received at least…I don't know what amount of consideration he wants or believes he's not gotten, but I want him to feel comfortable that at least he's had a fair, a fair hearing, a fair shot with a lawyer who has his best interests in mind. I don't believe he, obviously, feels that way now. If he wants to represent himself, and I've heard rumblings to that effect, that's okay with me, too. And I would be more than happy to assist him. I do know that Mr. Burgess has made arrangements for other counsel if the Court would allow that substitution."

"Other counsel is not here," Johnson asked from his high perch.

"The other counsel isn't here, but other counsel would be willing to appear by phone, Judge."

"Is he ready to appear on Monday morning?"

"That I…I don't know. You would have to ask him."

Blythe tried to say something. He got as far as. "I've talked to Mr. Custis and…."

But all Johnson cared about was that, "Mr. Custis has never had a case in the history that he's appeared before this Court that he's not requested continuance after continuance." Blythe managed to blurt that Custis might be ready to try the case in another month.

Barrett thought, "Thirty to 45 days. Mr. Anderson would be…have his time off and his refreshing, his vacation completed. You know, as…it seems to me…I know this matter has been continued a couple times, and part of what's gone on is motions, but it, honestly, seems that if Mr. Burgess wants other counsel and another 45 days, that seems little enough to ask if it's going to result in his feeling that he's gotten the process and the due process and the fairness that he deserves. I'm not going to respond at this stage directly to any of the allegations that I've heard other than to say that not only myself but others in the office have put in a number of hours reviewing this case, thinking through the facts, frankly, brainstorming defenses and approaches and any number of things. This is a circumstantial evidence case. It's a possession case. Whether it's pornography, whether it's drugs, whether it's a big rock from Yellowstone National Park, what it boils down to is possession, and that's what the defense boils down to is lack of knowledge, lack of knowledge of possession.

"If, if some of the evidence to be presented by the Government is such that...and I don't know, he can say I haven't seen it. I don't disagree with it. He can say I didn't know it was there. I don't disagree with that. I guess what I'm trying to figure out is what looking at it, although we have looked at the materials, what looking at it does to advance the case is very little, at least from the defendant's point of view, other than to satisfy himself I suppose that, yeah, these are not very appropriate photos."

Barrett who had defended multiple child porn cases had absolutely idea that exculpatory information might be found through a forensic examination of the evidence. He had no idea.

"But he's never...Mr. Burgess never has and I suspect never will come to the conclusion, and rightly so, that he was ever aware of his possession or ever having seen or having anything to do with this, these images. So that's where I am. I'm here at the Court's pleasure and the Court's discretion, and I'm more than happy to serve Mr. Burgess the best way I can. He may, he may not be happy and may never be, but all I can do is tell this Court and Mr. Burgess I'll do my best on his behalf. But if that's not good enough and he can't communicate and all that faith is gone, then I want him taken care of in that respect as well. And that seems little enough to ask. Thank you."

Anderson argued that the trial couldn't be delayed because too many people would be inconvenienced if it was. "Judge, the Government is ready to go to trial Monday morning. For the Court's information, will have I believe seven witnesses: A witness from Evanston, a trooper; a witness from Green River, DCI agent; FBI agent from Reno, Nevada; FBI agent from St. Louis. The FBI agent from St. Louis, really tough to book. She's going to identify a series of the images on the computer hard drive and identify them from a certain series that she investigated, a case that she investigated. And she's also booked to be in Minneapolis next week as well. To continue the trial would greatly inconvenience the Government. I can tell the Court that Mr. Barrett and Mr. Brinkerhoff both have been in contact with the Government over the course of this case on numerous occasions. Mr.

Brinkerhoff has been to the ICAC offices on six separate occasions to review the evidence in this particular case. I got that information today from the ICAC folks. Mr. Barrett has been out on three separate occasions to view the evidence. We have the evidence marked and labeled, and we are ready to make that available for inspection anytime between now and when the trial starts or any time during the trial that the defense so requests. We have opened up our files to the defense in every way we possibly can."

Anderson also thought Burgess was being unreasonable with Anderson's favorite public defender. "And, quite frankly," Anderson said, "I've always regarded Mr. Barrett as the finest...one of the finest practitioners if not the finest practitioner of defense, criminal defense in the District. And so I don't know that a substitution of counsel is going to do anything to advance the defendant's cause given the quality of counsel he already has. Whether the complexity of this action or any other relevant factors necessitate a delay. Judge, this is a simple case. It's a possession case, just like Mr. Barrett said, whether or not the defendant knowingly possessed a particular item, whether or not the defendant knowingly transported a particular item, that is, a couple of hard drives, across a state line. Pretty simple."

There were a couple of dryly humorous conversations with Dion Custis' answering machine before Burgess was finally invited to say what he thought.

*****

Dave Burgess said:

"I've never spoken like this before, so it's not going to be easy, but I'd like to kind of address the issues that the prosecution has to say about a couple of things.

"First of all, why am I doing this so late? The last time that I was in your court was on March 3rd, and on March the 3rd my pretrial services...or actually before I came up here my pretrial services person in Nevada asked me to speak with my attorney and get my home incarceration changed to home detention because I had discussed with him your concern about whether or not I am gonna need to pay for this, for my attorney. And so I asked him, I said, you know, I need to get out and start going and knocking on doors and talking to people to see if I can get, like, a defense fund together or something like that. And his answer to me was that, well you know, if I let you out like this, I'm sticking my neck out because you're on home incarceration, and home incarceration means you can make court dates, you can go to church, and you can go to the doctor.

"So he suggested that I talk to Mr. Barrett and get something filed with the court to get that modified. When I was here on March 3rd, Mr. Brinkerhoff spoke with...I believe, both Mr. Baker in Nevada, he's my pretrial guy, and also the pretrial guy here, and between March 3rd and March 5th they agreed that my home detention should be modified. When I left here on March 3rd, Mr. Barrett told me, he says, I'll take care of that for you.

"The following Friday I called my pretrial services guy in Nevada and asked him if he could check if I could get out. And he did check, and he said there's nothing in the court. And this was, I believe this was late on...this may have been late on Thursday. On Friday morning I talked with Mr. Barrett, and I asked Mr. Barrett what had happened about my...." That was as far as Burgess got before Barrett interrupted him to tell the court that Dion Custis was finally on the phone.

All Judge Johnson wanted to know was, "Are you ready to proceed on Monday?"

"I am not ready to proceed on Monday, no."

"Thank you. I don't have any further questions."

Then Burgess was allowed to continue and the months of frustration began to pour out.

"Okay. So one week later when I called Mr. Barrett and I asked him about what's the disposition of my modification of my terms of my bail or my bond, his exact words to me was 'I dropped the ball, I'll get on it right now.' I said, okay, that's fine. I called my pretrial service person back in Nevada, and he told me, well, we'll give him a few days to do this and then he'll check. I gave him another five days. I called back on that...I actually called my pretrial service guy on the following Friday, and I asked him, um, well, is there anything in the court yet, and he said no. I called Mr. Barrett back, either that or I believe he might have called me that morning, and that was about some other things, but the question I had for him is, has he put in the motion to modify. And I told him that both my pretrial service person in Nevada and the pretrial service person in Wyoming agreed that my

94

condition should be modified. He said, no, I'll get right on it. The same thing happened the third…for the third time. The reason that I needed to get out is because I remember I was sitting here when you were…had…you had reserved your decision on whether I was going to have to pay for this or not myself. I needed to get out in my neighborhood and talk to everyone I know to see if I could get some kind of money together. There was no way I could get out of my house. I was like a…you know, I was imprisoned in my own house. I couldn't get out. Um….."

"You have no phone," the judge asked.

"Yes, sir, I do have a phone, but a lot of the people that when I called, like, some business owners, um, I'd leave a message, and I wouldn't hear anything back. I know that I was definitely having problems because my telephone was hooked up to my leg monitor. Anybody that would call my house, you hear a big buzz comes in. So whether they would just hang up or not, I don't know. I needed to get out on the street, and I would have done that. Okay. Finally….."

"Anybody else could go out for you?"

"No, I live by myself in my house. So it's…there really wasn't too much I could do. I was just trying to get to where I could get out, and that way at least…and if…and I'll tell you, after….."

"No friends or associates?"

Burgess did not understand why Johnson was so contemptuous of him. The simple and obvious fact is, rather than simply being an arbiter, the passive aggressive, old bastard advocated against Burgess throughout the case. "Excuse me?" Burgess had always been generous with his money. His prosperity had become part of his identity. He was proud to be a wealthy man. He hated playing the part of a beggar.

"You don't have any friends or associates?"

"Yeah, I have friends and associates, but not people that were gonna go…in other words…the people that would come over like, um, like neighbors that I know that would go and buy me groceries and things like that, that wouldn't be appropriate for them to go and ask somebody for money for me. I needed to go and talk to them myself, and I would have done that if I could get out. As a matter of fact, in the last two days I have noticed that my condition was changed to where I was…I could get out during the day, and in one day I've got two promissory notes, one for $10,000, one for $35,000, from people that I know that I've helped in the past in the neighborhood and that are now in business. I helped, you know, like when they were feeling struggling back in ten, 15 years ago, I loaned them money. Now they have businesses, and they've decided to help me out. And I could...I did that in one day. I know it's the eleventh hour now. So I couldn't go and find myself an attorney because I didn't have any money to. So once I at least got those two promissory notes, um, I had an extended family member who is familiar with a good attorney in the state of Nevada. His name is David Chesnoff, and David Chesnoff said he was willing to come on board, but he was right in the middle of something, and this was only yesterday, and he said there was no way he could make it to the court today. He called, um, oh, I believe it's either...it was Robert Jackson maybe in... or I don't know if it was Robert. Anyway, he called a local attorney here, and he said that it was Friday and that attorney, he couldn't get a hold of that attorney. And so I was between a rock and a hard place. I knew that I needed to come in here with an attorney.

"When I got this original charge, the person that owned the trailer is the one that found Mr. Custis for me, and he said he's willing to come on board and do this, but he would be my local counsel, and I have an attorney in the state of Nevada that I...that's said if he had five days to look at the schedule, because he's a very busy attorney in the state of Nevada, that he would see if he could fit it into his Schedule. And so he needed to look at what was going on in the case and he could make his decision in five days. And I'm like, well, I don't know if I have those five days. But, anyway, my biggest problem that I have is last...also on...you know, it's...I notice that every one of these documents in here in my case, every one of these documents have my name on it. Up until three days ago I was only forwarded one document, and that was by Gayle. I don't know her last name. She works in Mr. Barrett's office. She sent me a copy of the motion to suppress. At that time I asked her, I said, well, I would like to have copies of everything. Um, here it is now, I'm standing here now, I still have never.... I've received not even one document from the prosecution's side. And I just noticed I was looking through the...all the documents. There are 16 documents total. Out of those 16 documents I have received five of them. And I received one of them right before I came to...into your hearing on March 3rd, and I received the other four in the last

96

two days for what's even going on.

"And I have a complete record here of all of my e-mails that...with my correspondence with Gayle, and the problem that I'm having here, you know, it's.... I mean, I don't know if Mr. Barrett is busy with other things, but Mr. Barrett told me that he dropped the ball. I've been in court for, I would say, every day in civil matters for the last 20 years. I've never had an attorney tell me he's dropped the ball ever. And, I've had locally in the Nevada area and California probably upwards of over 20 attorneys on civil cases.

"And the first time when he told me that he dropped the ball, I...you know, I mean, I was leery about it at that time. That's why I was really motivated to get out and see if I could get an attorney in my neighborhood that would help me out on this thing. And it went up.... Two more times I called him in a three-week period, and he still didn't.... I mean, this was something that's simple. I'm looking at this document here for this defendant's motion for modification. It's one page, and then, of course, the little signing sheet on the back. And on here it says that both...it says it's approved by both Wyoming pretrial services and by the defendant's supervisor in the state of Nevada. That was approved on somewhere between. March 3rd and March 7th. This document, urn, was given to the Court on April 7th. I was stuck at my house more than a month when I should have been out on the street finding myself what...you .know, an attorney that's gonna at least keep me apprised of what's going on.

"And the whole thing about this is, even with Gayle, like I said, I've talked to her a couple of times on the telephone, but she started religiously e-mailing me everything on...I don't know what today is. Today is the 11th...on the 9th of April, trying to tell me what's, trying to tell me what's going on. And I would like to read this into the...for the Court to listen to."

"Sure," the judge said.

Dave Burgess, the Hells Angel, seemed to have the naïve delusion that the judge cared. He had born all his frustrations with Barrett stoically. Now he hoped he had found a judge who would understand the injustices that had been done to him, so he tried to explain that his lawyer had ignored him and his case. "Okay. So that's what I'm gonna do right now. Okay. The first one I received on March, I mean, on April 9th in the morning from her, from Gayle, and it's...what this is, is it says: See attached file, defendant's motion for continuance. Okay. That's what I received from Gayle. Okay? And that was in the...that morning. Okay?

"Then I, what I did is I immediately wrote her right back, I emailed her right back: Sorry, Gayle, none of the attachments came through. Thank you, David Burgess.

"Number three is she...number three she sent me the motion for a continuance, okay, and that's what I received, I just received the...my attorney's motion for the continuance of the trial, and so I wrote this back to her: 'Greetings, Gayle. The motion of continuance...the motion came through, but the order did not, so I do not know when the new trial date is.'

"She writes me back again, um, the next...the following morning. It says: 'I'll try again in a different format. Jim is at the court talking to the Judge about the continuance. I'll let you know as soon as I know about when your trial will be continued. Your motion for modification of bond was signed. Will be in touch with you shortly. Gayle.'

"Okay. The next thing that came by was she wrote me again, and she said: 'Jim and the AUSA (Anderson, the Assistant United States Attorney) are at a meeting with the Judge in the morning at 9:30 a.m. regarding the continuance of the trial. I'll let you know as soon as I do. Here are some motions that were filed today. Thanks, Gayle.'

"Okay. I wrote her right back as soon as I read that, that...again I said: 'Greetings again, Gayle. The motions did not come through. The attachments did not come through.'

"Okay. Then she sent me another...then she sent me another e-mail, which was the...it was...what she sent me next was a motion denying, the motion denying the suppression. And she sent me that and also a copy of the order granting continuance, which was I guess moot at that point, but those two came together. And she sent a little note along with this. It says: 'He has not granted the continuance. Just received the motion denying suppression. Jim hasn't even seen it yet. I'll be in touch. Thanks, Gayle.'

"Then she sent me another e-mail on the 10th of April: 'We have a trial on Monday, Dave. Do you have any names, addresses, and potential witnesses? Jim will meet with you on Sunday at 3 p.m. here at the office. Please let me know that you received this.'" The week before the trial, Barrett still had no idea what his defense would be or what witnesses or evidence he would need to support that defense. Barrett left all that up to Burgess and Dave's faithful friend, Troy Regas. And, Barrett suggested that they brief him 15 hours before the trial was scheduled to begin.

"I immediately sent her back a list of my witnesses," Burgess rushed on, as if Judge Johnson might again grow impatient with this long tale he of woe he had to tell. "Okay, plus I sent two more amendments where I added people onto that in the same day. And that was the next thing. Okay?

"And then the final thing that I got from her, which was on the 10th, says: 'Please give Steve a call so you can discuss what they will be testifying to. Thanks, Gayle.'

"Now, today is the 11th. Yesterday was the 10th. This is when I'm receiving, finally receiving this stuff.

"Now, I have…. I admit that I talked…on the morning or the day that I was in here on the 3rd, okay? Mr. Brinkerhoff says you need to start getting a witness list together. And I did start getting a witness list together. But at that point in the next few days this whole thing came up about getting my home detention modified so I can get out there and start to see if I can drum up some money so I could get myself, you know…. Like if…because at that point you sat up there and said I'm gonna reserve my…."

"Actually, I really didn't say any of that," Johnson told Burgess. Burgess had waited months to finally begin to tell his story to someone. In reply, Johnson bullied Burgess from the bench. The pop psychologist Eric Berne called these sorts of exchanges "crossed transactions." Burgess hoped Johnson would recognize the accused man's plight and help him. Johnson wanted to shift the blame for Barrett's incompetence from Barrett to Burgess.

"You didn't say that you were gonna…."

"Here's the transcript of that hearing." It was a heartless stunt for a federal district judge to pull on a man who only wanted a fair trial. Now Burgess had another court document to read that he had never seen before.

"Okay. Well, that's…what I heard is…did you say that I could have one? Or you said you were waiting for some information."

"Actually, Mr. Barrett didn't drop the ball at all." Johnson studied Burgess from his high place. "It says here…. Johnson read from the transcript: 'Mr. Barrett – Mr. Burgess has asked, and I don't know if you're the person to approach about it, but as long as we have Mr. Anderson here, I cannot confirm this absolutely, but I believe there's been some communication between the supervising officer in Nevada, Mr. Burgess' supervising officer, and pretrial services here in Wyoming.'"

"Okay."

"'And they have suggested," Johnson droned Barrett's long and confused statements, "'because Mr. Burgess has requested a little flexibility to take care of business that one of his conditions be changed to home detention.'" The Judge Johnson managed to restrain himself from saying out loud, "Now I got you, you son of a bitch!" Then he continued, "There's no mention there of any problem with attorneys or that the business was seeking an attorney or anything other than business. Is that right?"

Burgess tried to answer. "That's...."

"I probably stuck the piece of paper in here," Johnson continued to read from the transcript Burgess had never and would never see, as if the issue was the authority of the court rather than Barrett's inadequacy as a defender. 'But that his bond conditions be modified to home detention...which it was...."

"But, but...."

"'...which would allow him to leave his...' ah, here we are! This is a recommendation coming from the supervisor in Nevada? That's my question. It's, it's...the supervisor in Nevada has been consulted and has no objection and Mr. Brinkerhoff contacted her, but I'm not party to the conversation, so I need to...' Johnson quoted Barrett. Then he quoted himself. 'And I interrupt: Why don't you let me...or would you look into it with....'"

Johnson continued to read from the transcript of the hearing, defending Barrett and blaming Burgess. He quoted Barrett, " I need to verify it, but I think that's what the request would be, just a modification from home incarceration to home detention, which would restrict Mr. Burgess' travel and contacts to his residence at all times except for employment, education, religious services, medical, substance abuse treatments, attorney visits, court appearances, and the like. That would allow him to participate a little more directly in his business.'

"" What is it now," the Judge quoted Anderson as asking.

Then he quoted himself again, "I say, 'I'll call the court and inquire.' Alright'" Barrett had said. "'Thank you judge.' And that was about it."

Burgess remembered the March 3rd hearing, the hearing on suppressing the evidence seized from the Freightliner. "Okay. Well, I agree with what you said there. I remember that now. And so that was on the 3rd of March. Okay. Also that same day, though, I know that before we left here something came up because I believe you asked Mr. Anderson something about, um, there was…they were waiting for something from the Internal Revenue Service, some kind of documents. I don't know, but it was something…."

"That's correct," the judge interrupted.

The increasingly discombobulated Burgess, struggled to maintain his composure. "…to see, okay, if I could…was gonna have…. So that alerted me right then that I was thinking I need to see if I can find some, get some money somewhere to get maybe to…if I'm gonna have to get my own attorney. Okay? I couldn't get my own attorney because I'm stuck at my house. It says I wasn't…I can't go and see…have attorney visits. So I can't even go and visit an attorney. So but, anyway, the bottom line of this whole thing is that all happened…."

"Well," Johnson interrupted again.

: …on March 3rd. Okay? The document that Mr. Barrett gave to the Court, he gave to the Court on the 7th of April. That was over a month later. And I'm going to court here in three days." Burgess began to sputter. "And I mean, who's…I mean, I don't know, it's…I don't know who to blame here, but the bottom line is, is I should have been out looking for an attorney and doing what I needed to do. In other words, what happened…in the beginning I wasn't going out to find a new attorney because I didn't have a problem with Mr. Barrett. I had a problem with Mr. Barrett when Mr. Barrett told me he dropped the ball. Okay? Now, I know that you are reading what you are reading there. Mr. Barrett told me he, dropped the ball, and he did say that to me. And you can ask him yourself. And you can also ask him how many times did I call him and ask him when is this gonna happen. And the reason that I kept asking him was because I kept getting a bad time from my pretrial guy in Nevada. He says, I'm too busy to do your homework for you. If you want to have this thing changed, you need to get your attorney in Wyoming to do it. He says he has already discussed it with the pretrial person in the state of Wyoming, they both agreed. The next step was Mr. Barrett needs to give the Court some kind of a document that could be signed to let me do this. It did happen. It happened on the 7th of April. Okay? And that's over a month later. And in the three weeks going up to that I'm thinking to myself, if he, if he won't do that, what is he doing for me? And...."

Johnson continued to toy with Burgess. "What day did you tell Mr. Barrett?"

"That day when I was in here on the 3rd of March."

"And you said, I'm not gonna have you as my attorney?"

"Oh, no, no, no, no."

"I'm gonna fire you?"

"No. Excuse me."

"And I'm gonna hire somebody else?"

"No, no. I haven't even seen Mr. Barrett. Mr. Barrett hasn't been available. I'm telling you he hasn't been available for me."

The judge was skeptical. "Since March 3rd?"

"No, no, this didn't happen on March 3rd. I didn't have a problem with him on March 3rd. Okay?"

"Well, you wanted to get another attorney."

Burgess continued on in his naïve believe that federal justice is just and that federal judges want to do the just thing. 'Not on March 3rd. What I wanted to do was I wanted to be ready in case you said that I needed to pay for this. I needed money. So if I'm gonna have to pay money, I figured I might as well go...if I'm gonna have...if I get money together, I'm gonna go see if I can at least get an attorney that's in my area that I can be able to visit every day because this is an important thing for me. I mean, heck, it's my whole life."

"Sure it is. Why weren't you in touch with your attorney? I didn't...you had a trial date." Johnson continued to act as if he didn't know that Barrett had been on vacation for two of the three weeks leading up to Burgess' trial.

"I was in touch with my attorney. I kept calling my...I called my attorney three separate occasions just for that, just for that particular thing is when am I gonna get a little adjustment here, because at that point I'm still wondering about, am I gonna have to pay for this. You know, that's a big thing. I mean, also it is my life, but if I gotta pay for it, I have to pay for it, and I can't go out and do any of that stuff. Your Honor, I gotta tell you, Mr. Barrett told me he dropped the ball. When an attorney tells me that he dropped the ball, what else am I supposed to think?"

Johnson continued to refuse to understand. "Well, you're supposed to ask him questions."

"I did ask him questions."

"What questions did you ask him?"

"I asked him, How come you haven't done it? He says, I'll get on...."

"Done what?"

"How come that...how come that we have not put the motion to suppress...I mean, excuse me, the motion...how come we haven't put the motion to have my bail modified in the...."

"That's the whole ball that was dropped, right?" Johnson refused to hear that Barrett didn't talk to Burgess for months on end. He deflected Burgess' complaints. It is harder to understand why. The entire exchange suggests that Johnson had already judged the case.

"Excuse me?"

"That's it. That's the ball he dropped?"

"That's the ball he dropped, but he dropped it three times." Burgess was so flustered by Johnson that he would say anything to try to find some agreement with the judge.

"Alright."

"He dropped it three times. You know, and it's.... I'm thinking if he's gonna drop the ball on that three times, what else is going on? Okay?" Burgess probably understood how helplessly lost he was then – at that point in the hearing – but he continued to try to make the heartless judge understand that he was innocent, that he hoped to prove it but his lawyer wouldn't help him.

"How come I haven't until two days ago seen any...I mean, every one of these documents has my name on it. I asked the secretary for copies of it. I never received it until starting on the...when you denied the motion to suppress is when I started receiving stuff. It was like all of a sudden then it became important, but up until that time it was like it was only...I was an inconvenience. You know, and I'm telling you, I don't think I'm getting a fair shake here. If I have to go to trial on Monday, I don't think I'm gonna be represented the way that I should be represented. I mean, I've talked to a few attorneys in the state of Nevada. They said that wouldn't happen there. My pretrial guy said that. I says...when we asked for a modification, they get the modification within one week. And, of course, my pretrial guy is blaming me for it. He says, 'That's your thing. You're the one that needs to take care of that.'

"I said, 'I've tried.' I've talked to Mr. Barrett on...you know, this is...every time I said this to him. I said, I've asked him to do it, it's not getting done, and I...at this point I don't know what else I can do. Finally on the 7th of April he put it in, but I didn't get a copy of that until the 9th.

"Your Honor, I need to get myself another attorney, and I have another attorney, David Chesnoff, in the state of Nevada that would like to go forward with this and using the local counsel here, Mr., um, Mr. Custis. But I don't see how I can go to trial...I mean, I want to be prepared to go to trial. This is my whole life. I'm looking at 20 years in prison for something I didn't do. You know, I need to be able to defend myself. I need experts. Who...I don't have any...I don't even...I don't know if I have any experts, you know. I've talked to Mr. Brinkerhoff. He says, 'Well, they have an expert.' To me it almost seems like the experts are the experts the Government has. I need my own experts. I need my own people to look at each and every one of these things to see what they are. You know, I'll tell you, in the beginning, even up till probably the 15th of March, I was still confident in Mr. Barrett. I mean, I gave him the one...he dropped the ball one time. Okay, you dropped it one time. But he dropped it two more times after that.

"I mean, I don't know what else to say here. I mean, it's.... If I thought I was gonna get a fair shake and if I thought that everybody had all their tees crossed and their eyes dotted, it would be okay. And that's another problem I have. You know, when I turn my homework in, I make sure that everything is spelled right. I know that you have read stuff that came from the public defender's office that have...the words are jumbled up in it. You know, I mean, to me that's just.... You know, I don't know, to me that seems like a courtesy to the Court to make sure when you turn something in that the judge has to read that he's being educated and he's also reading something that makes sense. He doesn't have to say, oh, well, he meant this word.

"I'll tell you, Your Honor, I don't know what to do at this point. I've lost confidence in my counsel. And, you know, I'm not a public speaker. Um, I'm in the position now...it's

104

not my money. You know, that's another thing. Mr. Anderson says, 'How come all of a sudden he's got money for this?' The only reason I have money for this is because two days ago I was let to where I could go out and start rattling doors, and people are now starting to come around. They're seeing me, 'Oh, gee you're…Gee, we didn't…' You know? So you're here? Because these aren't people that I see on an everyday basis. These are people that I've known over the years and they're willing to help me out. And I'm telling you, they're willing to help me out.

"A business owner up the street from where I live, I mean, I have it right here, it says, 'This is a note of surety…' or 'this note is a surety note for the sum of $35,000. This note shall be given to the bearer of this note at day and time to be given in the defense and on behalf of David Burgess,' signed Bobby McDowell. It has his, his business address, his home phone number, and his, and his cell number on it. And I have another one here that says the same thing for $10,000. I did that in one day, you know. And I called my in-laws, and I said, um, I have people that I've talked to now, and they're gonna get a defense fund for me together. And we need to hire the most competent attorney we can for this. This is the rest of my life. Not only that is, if I'm convicted of this and I become a felon, I lose my business license in a business that I've been trying to build for almost 30 years and it goes down the drain in one day.

"I wouldn't do something as stupid as what I'm accused of here, you know. I mean, I understand the business that I'm in and not everybody agrees with it. And I'll tell you what. There's a lot of federal people that have a vendetta against me. And they are willing to do a lot of things. I don't know if you have looked at any of my record, but they took my business license away when I wanted to become a Hells Angel.

"You know, they completely violated my Second Amendment. I took it to court. I won. I'm still…. I'm back in business, plus they had to pay me for all the time I was out. You know, there's certain things you can't do. But I'll tell you what, the government in that particular instance was not above making me pay. You know, it's always one way or the other. You know, let's…. I've been having problems with the Internal Revenue Service not for my taxes but for the girls' taxes that work at my establishments. Why would they come after me for that? Because they can. I'm the one with the pockets.

"Your Honor, I need to get...have myself counsel that can represent me in this case or I'm finished. And I've lost confidence in my attorney, and I don't know what else to tell you. You know, I don't want to get upset or anything like that, but this is the rest of my.... This is my life, you know.

"I'm willing to come through...to this...to everything. You know that I'm gonna show up at this. I'm not that kind of person that would give my word and then run off. But I want to be represented by somebody that I have confidence in, and I have lost confidence in my counsel." On and on Burgess begged, at one point close to breaking down and weeping. And Judge Johnson regarded him coldly and impassively.

"And I don't know what else to tell you, you know. I mean, I'm not stalling. I'm not doing any of those things. I want to be able to sit down with my counsel and know exactly what the Government has, what the Government has been saying, what the Government's been doing. All those records, I've never seen those until today. There are 16 documents there. I have received five of them. I received four of them in the last two days. You know, these things have my name on them. That's...to me that seems like they're addressed to me. Somebody could give me the courtesy when they got them to at least CC them to me. They had my email address.

"You know, I sure would just like the chance to be able to defend myself, Your Honor. I don't know what else to say. I don't. I guess I don't have anything else to say. I'll sit down, if you want me to."

"Thank you," Johnson said. Then he completely ignored Burgess' impassioned plea for justice and went back to quoting from the transcript Burgess had never seen. "Another point to be raised in terms of the transcript of the March 3rd hearing. The Court stated: 'Alright. There are two things that are kind of on the plate here. One is the issue of representation, which has never been resolved by the Court. I think we're waiting for some examination from the Government.'

"Mr. Anderson replies: 'We're waiting for something from the IRS. I haven't gotten anything yet.'

"Mr. Barrett says: 'I've had a communication from the IRS but not with regard to that matter.'

"'Alright. Well, you know, time's passing'" Johnson quoted himself.

Then he quoted Barrett. "'I know. I'm just...Mr. Burgess and I are just simply proceeding.'

And then he quoted himself again. "'My inclination is that, you know, at some point if we don't hear, that issue is going to pass, and we'll deal with it in terms of considering at the end of the case, whatever happens, what compensation should be...should, if any, be paid by Mr. Burgess for your services.'"

And, then Johnson went on to tell Dave Burgess that ultimately Burgess was responsible for his own defense; and that he, not Barrett had dropped the ball.

"The court must balance a defendant's constitutional right to retain counsel of choice against the need to maintain the highest standards of professional responsibility, the public's confidence in the integrity of the judicial process, and the orderly administration of justice. In weighing this balance courts may consider whether a continuance to allow one's preferred attorney to handle the case would inconvenience witnesses, the court, counsel, or the parties, whether other continuances have been granted, whether legitimate reasons exist for the delay, or whether the defendant contributed to the circumstances which gave rise to the request for continuance. Similarly, the court may consider whether defendant had other competent counsel prepared to try the case, with attention to whether defendant obtained the other counsel as lead or associate counsel, whether rejecting defendant's request for delay will result in identifiable prejudice to his case, whether this prejudice constitutes a material or substantial harm, whether the complexity of the action or other relevant factors peculiar to the specific case necessitates further delay.

"This case actually started in July of 2007 with a stop on a Wyoming highway. Frankly, I believe the Wyoming Highway Patrol was on the lookout for the, the vehicle anyway, which was recognized as a vehicle associated with Hells Angels. I'm not sure I remember why it was on the lookout, but it seems to me they had received some information that the vehicle would be passing through, the motor home with the trailer attached. And, sure enough, as I recall, the officer was at JB's having a cup of coffee in the morning, looks out the door, and there, there it is. And runs license checks and finds that the license had expired with regard to the trailer that was being pulled. It turned out the trailer was...had been lent or was owned by somebody in...an organization in Wamsutter that had failed to have the license brought up."

Judge Johnson knew all his words were being transcribed and were likely to appear in some future appeal so he spoke to those appeals judges. He wasn't really talking to Dave Burgess.

"At any rate, a dog sniff generated enough cause that a search ensued for controlled substances and the officers found them. And this case ultimately commenced with a prosecution follow indictment that occurred on November 14th, 2007 with the defendant having counsel appointed by the 20th of November, 2007. There have been other continuances granted in this case, and the Court was fairly lenient with regard to those, those requests. But at its base this case is rather straightforward. The issue of the suppression. is one that has its unique set of facts. The defense relied heavily upon a case called *Carey* that involved, in my view, a different…was distinguishable. But that is neither here nor there. The Tenth Circuit has found me wrong upon occasion and has agreed with me upon occasion, and that issue was preserved forevermore for consideration on appeal should an appeal follow in this matter.

"From his first notification…and I was just going to check here…well, the Rule Five hearing occurred with Mr. Burgess on November 26th, 2007 in Nevada. So certainly he was aware of the nature of the indictment or the charges against him at that time, if he wasn't aware, and on the street between July 2007 and November of 2007. Certainly an adequate opportunity to prepare private counsel, line them up and prepare people to be ready to respond should anything materialize from Wyoming and it eventually did in November.

"What eventually occurred in August of 2007 was through an appropriate examination by Special Agent Hughes for drug information on the computers a JPEG image of child pornography was noted, and immediately the investigation was shut down and another search warrant was obtained, and this information developed with regard to child pornography. That involved the search of hard drives that were seized by law enforcement when the motor home was seized by them in July of 2007. Those hard drives have been examined, and the information relating to the charges here as contained in the Indictment have been developed.

"This case is not one that has the complexity of others that we try in this court on a fairly frequent basis where there is a computer program for file sharing, such as LimeWire or BearWare. Those shareware programs, of course, create a level of complexity that doesn't exist here." Johnson was referring to all the other child pornography cases investigated by the Cheyenne ICAC Task Force. In every other child pornography case, the sleuths at ICAC had witnessed an internet exchange of child pornography between two computers before proceeding with the rest of the investigation. Dave Burgess case was unique. Child pornography had simply appeared on two hard drives that government agents had claimed belonged to him. But Judge Johnson didn't think that made Burgess case unique. He thought that made Burgess' case simple. So he continued:

"Rather the computer is, is like a, in a way, a person's residence. A lot of information is kept on a computer, both personal and otherwise, stored there because it is a marvelous instrument to store images and text information and make it usable. The issues in this case are straightforward. Did, in fact, this defendant possess those items knowingly that were on that computer? Of course, foundation has to be laid from an evidentiary standpoint that these items were, in fact, on the computer, and the Government will either succeed in that proof or fail in that proof. It is not particularly magic in that the jury is...would have to decide whether it believes the testimony of Special Agent Hughes after it listens to the processes that he went through in this, in this regard."

Johnson went ahead and laid out for Anderson would he would have to prove to secure Dave Burgess' conviction.

"And then, obviously, the question is: Are the surrounding facts and circumstances such to indicate that this defendant possessed these items, that it was his computer, it was his hard drive, that these images...would it be likely that he would know that these images were on the computer by what is there? And, of course, there's an issue of interstate transportation of this computer and the hard drives...."

On and on Judge Johnson outlined the reasons why, in his mind, Dave Burgess was obviously guilty. There would be no delay. The trial would proceed the following Monday as scheduled.

The Trial

On Sunday, the day before the trial would begin, Jim Barrett, the defense attorney Judge Johnson had told Dave Burgess he had to use unless Burgess was planning on defending himself, still hadn't written an opening statement, still hadn't interviewed any witnesses, still didn't know which witnesses he might call and he still hadn't hired anyone to forensically examine the child pornography that was the principal evidence against his client. He told Dave Burgess he still hadn't devised a defense strategy and he asked Burgess for suggestions. Burgess didn't know what to say except that he had no idea how the dirty pictures had appeared on his hard drives. When Troy Regas asked the lawyer what Dave's defense would be, Barrett replied, "Cops in Reno are bad, but the cops in Wyoming are good."

Barrett then told Regas that he intended to try a "new strategy." Barrett said he had decided not to give an opening statement until after the prosecution rested. Regas, asked if that was because Barrett didn't know what to say and Barrett admitted that he couldn't give an opening statement if he tried.

The day before the trial, seven of the defense witnesses Barrett would eventually call had not yet been subpoenaed but a dozen people had flown to Cheyenne at their own expense to support Dave. The potential witnesses included Yvonne Regas, Troy and Sohn Regas and their younger sister Fara Rials, and Rachael Curtis the girl whose photos had been obscenely captioned. Two other girls named Taylor Jennings and Leza Deshaies-Price who were with Rachael when the photographs were taken in a motel room in Winnemucca, Nevada also flew to Wyoming. Rebecca Deshaies, who was Dave Burgess' current girlfriend, the mother of Leza Deshaies-Price and Rachael Curtis' legal guardian, a woman who had been in the motel room in

Winnemucca when some of the "nude and semi-nude" photographs of Rachael were taken, had also flown to Wyoming to support Dave.

Barrett's investigator, Steve Brinkerhoff, briefly interviewed most of the potential witnesses. The most important of these was Steven Byars, the disabled Vietnam veteran who was Dave Burgess cousin and who had actually built and maintained Dave's website, *davesworld81*. Byars talked to both Brinkerhoff and Barrett and he was probably the most important potential witness in the case.

Byers was prepared to testify that he and Dave Burgess had purchased three hard drives together. The two men had bought one Maxtor and one Seagate portable hard drive. When the first Maxtor broke they bought a second Maxtor and Dave put the broken Maxtor in a drawer and left it there. The two men used the drives to constantly back up Dave's website. Dave would back up the site on the Seagate and then swap it out for the Maxtor. Byars would take physical possession of whichever hard drive was not in use and back it up. Byars looked at the drives regularly, and he never saw any pornography on any of them.

Byars, a programmer who designed computer security systems and databases, wanted Dave to secure his computers but Burgess had replied that he didn't want his computers secured because he wanted his friends to have easy access to the machines. Byars was also prepared to testify that although Dave Burgess supplied the content for *davesworld81*, he was not a sophisticated computer user. Byars wanted to testify that he had never found Burgess to be a particularly well organized man, that Dave never could have organized a database with tens of thousands of images and that *davesworld81* was an amateur, not professional site.

Byars wanted to examine the evidence against Burgess, which brought him into conflict with both Brinkerhoff and Barrett. Byars wanted to know whether the images had been added to the Maxtor all at once or piece meal and he wanted to run history tests on the images to see whether they had actually been moved around and organized, which is what Anderson was about to tell a jury.

That evening before the trial, Brinkerhoff told Byars that he wouldn't be allowed to testify, let alone examine the evidence. Because Byars had been diagnosed with post-traumatic stress disorder and because Byars passionately

111

believed that his cousin and friend was being framed, Barrett was afraid Byars might lose his temper on the stand and attack somebody – despite the fact that Byars was confined to a wheelchair.

The morning the trial began, Barrett did hire someone knowledgeable about computers to look at the evidence against Dave Burgess. Barrett hired Gene Jone, the then 35 year old Information Technology Administrator in the Denver Federal Public Defenders office. Jone had taken a course in using EnCase, but his principal duties were to install new computers and software. He was attending the trial anyway, because another of his duties was to assist federal defenders in making power point evidence presentations. Jone had moved to Denver from Guam four years before and the IT job in the public defenders office was simply a stop gap. In real life Jone was "DVDJ G-Funk," a "veteran DJ for two decades." According to his website, "DVDJ G-Funk programs all his mixes and mashups with videos from old-school, retro, hip-hop, electro and current hits so you can see and hear his live performance. This professional A/V artist never spins a dull moment as he entertains the crowd on and off the dance floor. DVDJ G-Funk is the future of DJ Entertainment and the Revolution of Digital Video Disc Jockeys. Seeing is Believing."

DVDJ G-Funk never examined the evidence against Dave Burgess until Thursday morning, four days into the trial but the trial proceeded on time anyway.

During jury selection on Monday morning, Judge Johnson made a point of telling the prospective jurors the two, most prejudicial things they would hear about Burgess.

"Mr. Barrett has informed us that the defendant a...owns or manages or is connected with a brothel, a house where there is prostitution, outside of Reno, Nevada. It is my understanding that under the laws of that State the brothel business may be lawful, subject to regulation by the State and paying of business taxes and having permits and that sort of thing. Would any of you have difficulty listening to this case and weighing the evidence on the charges against this defendant because of the occupation of this defendant? Does that represent a special problem to any of you?"

"The second area that I think might be of concern that's been raised here by Mr. Barrett is he has informed us that Mr. Burgess has in the past and for all I know still is a member of a motorcycle group called Hells Angels, which in the past has received negative publicity in newspapers, magazines, and I think maybe 30 or 40 years ago there was a movie with Henry Fonda's son, Peter, that painted kind of a...a negative portrait of Hells Angels. I don't have any knowledge one way or the other at this point concerning Hells Angels, but the real issue is: Would you be able to set aside any concern or notion you have about Hells Angels and decide this case on the facts that are presented during the trial? Any problem with that idea?"

After a jury was selected that had absolutely no prejudices towards Hells Angels, prostitution or Henry Fonda's son Peter, Barrett, Anderson and Johnson met outside its presence to discuss how many offensive or lewdly captioned photos Anderson would be allowed to shove in the jurors' faces.

"Your Honor," Anderson lied, "in regards to the map of the hard drive, Agent Hughes will testify today or early tomorrow that during the course of his examination of the defendant's hard drive he encountered approximately 166,000 images, 166,000 images. And he estimates...and he spent, he'll tell the Court, between 180 and 200 hours on his examination of the hard drive. Of those 166,000 images approximately 45 to 55 percent were either hard-core child pornography or child erotica. The map is not hearsay as defined by Rule 801. Hearsay is a statement other than one made by a declarant while testifying at trial or hearing offered in evidence to prove the truth of the matter asserted...."

Anderson talked at great length. "...and then if you get to Nastiest 1yoSeries, underneath that you'll find a bunch of the additional folders. Now, we didn't draw up the images, and we're not going to present the images to the jury of the images Sausage In the Ass, but I will represent to the Court that we looked at that folder last night; it shows an 11 year old girl with a sausage being inserted by her into her anus. The next one, Sausage In the...I will assert...I will represent to the Court that that represents an 11 year old girl inserting a sausage into her vagina. About 10 photographs in each. SausagePlay, again, shows a sausage being used by that 11 year old girl imitating fellatio and other things. The long and the short of it is, Judge, this is a road map to the nature, extent, and scope of the child pornography collection collected by the defendant, and it is not hearsay. It is simply that it's a road map. And while it may be prejudicial, it is not unfairly prejudicial because it was not the Government that created this document. It was the owner of that Maxtor hard drive."

"It looks to me," Anderson continued, "like the defense in this matter is going to be two things, a shoddy investigation and also the SODDI defense, "Some Other Dude Did It." If that's the case, Judge, certainly the organization of the defendant's child pornography collection will have a great bearing upon the issue of knowledge, the issue of whether or not there was knowing possession."

"Judge, again, the defendant is arguing...I believe the defendant is going to argue some other dude did it, I don't know anything about this. If you look at the highly structured and organized fashion of this map and how this stuff is split out, it's hard to imagine anybody that's created a document like this or a structure like this that would not, would not know what's within those folders."

It might seem that the point of the trial was to decide whether "the owner of that Maxtor hard drive" had actually placed the pornography on the drive or whether the people who had possessed the drive for 44 days – and stored it in a library of child pornography after Burgess last saw it – had put the offensive pictures there. There might also be some minimal discussion of some proof that connected Burgess to the drive. The thing had never been fingerprinted.

But Johnson did not see the case that way. "Well," he began, "I'm not necessarily of a mind to exclude it. I don't agree with Jim Barrett. A computer directory – Cheryl handed me a case here, *United States against Aoki Lee*...a Ninth Circuit case again: A computer directory is like a card in an old-fashioned library catalog, that tells where to find a book on a shelf."

"That's the exact analogy we're going to use for the jury this morning in PowerPoint," Anderson enthused.

"Sure," Johnson ruled. "That is not hearsay."

Barrett just stood there and let the judge and the prosecutor get away with it.

"Well, as I understand it," Johnson checked with Anderson, "from the Government's standpoint or what you've told me, there were 166,000 separate files or...no, separate images...."

"Correct!"

"...contained in the files reflected in the 23 pages of the map and 45 percent of those or roughly 70,000 were

114

images of children under the age of 8 years. Am I correct?"

And Anderson assured Johnson, exactly as Ed McMahon had once agreed with Johnny Carson, "You are correct Judge!"

After deciding the preliminary issue of whether or not Dave Burgess had obsessively catalogued approximately 31,500 pornographic images of children under eight years old on what had to have been his hard drive, the trial was ready to begin.

*****

Anderson's carefully conceived and rehearsed, 3,500 word opening statement took about 25 minutes to deliver.

"You'll hear testimony that a highway patrolman by the name of Matt Arnell stopped them. Matt Arnell stopped them. There was a search. There was a subsequent search of that motor home, and that computer equipment was found in that motor home. There was a laptop, and there were two external hard drives."

"That equipment was turned over to DCI agents. That stands for Wyoming Division of Criminal Investigation, our state police force. They were transported back here to Cheyenne, where they were subsequently examined. And that examination revealed just an almost unimaginable amount of child pornography on those hard drives. When I talk about child pornography, please don't misunderstand. I'm not talking about images of 15, 16, 17 year old girls in lascivious poses. We're talking about crime scene photographs of young children being treated in a way that no child should ever be treated."

"We're gonna call a number of witnesses, and the first witness that we're gonna call is a fella by the name of Trooper Matt Arnell. He's a Wyoming highway patrolman. He's been a patrolman for seven years. And Trooper Arnell on the morning of July 24th of 2007 was on duty, and, gee, I know none of you have ever had this happen during the course of your experience, but he was parked in front of a coffee shop having a cup of coffee. Now, I know that that sounds unusual, but there he was in front of a coffee…at a coffee shop having a cup of coffee, probably another couple of cop cars there. They're having coffee, and out the window he looks, and what does he see but a number motorcycles and this big motor home. And Trooper Arnell will tell you that he had been put on alert about that motorhome because he knew it belonged to the Hells Angels. He knew that there was a Hells Angels rally going to be going on over in the Midwest someplace, I believe in Arkansas."

"And he went out, and he took a look at that motor home, and he looked at a trailer that it was towing. And, interestingly enough, that trailer – the motor home was registered out in Nevada, but it had a trailer that was registered or it was supposed to be registered in Wyoming, but the registration had expired. Trooper Arnell took note of that."

Barrett didn't make an opening statement because he was trying out a new trial strategy he had never tried before – of letting the fella that was the judge, and the fellas and gals of the jury and the fella who was the defendant guess for a couple of days what Burgess' defense was gonna be.

So Anderson leapt right into questioning Arnell. The prosecution established that Burgess was an admitted drug user who was travelling in a "war wagon." The war wagon was so notorious that police were looking for it. And, Arnell let the war wagon drive out of town before he stopped it because he was afraid there might be a shootout at the cluster of motels and gas stations. Eventually, through meticulous police work, Arnell discovered the Maxtor drive hidden in Dave Burgess' couch.

"And you didn't put the Maxtor in the, down in that couch" Anderson told Arnell.

And Arnell agreed, "No, I did not."

Since there were some incriminating things Anderson had forgotten to bring up, Barrett asked Arnell if any weapons were found in the war wagon. And, Arnell was able to reply that there were three knives, one of which had a 12 inch blade. Barrett wasn't able to work into the conversation that the drug charges had all been dropped against both Waldron and Burgess. But he did invite Arnell to talk about the marijuana that had been found in a duffle bag.

Then on redirect, Anderson slipped in the innuendo that while Arnell and Waldron were retrieving the trailer registration, Burgess had been hiding the Maxtor hard drive "chock-full" of child porn inside the springs of his couch.

"Just a couple of questions," Anderson began. "From the time that you stopped the motorhome until Mr. Burgess exited the motorhome, approximately how much time elapsed?

"Uh, five minutes, as a guess."

"Do you know what Mr. Burgess was doing in that motor home during that five-minute period?"

"I do not."

Arnell was dismissed, although he did stay to attend the rest of the trial, and Barrett called two defense character witnesses out of order. They were Dave Burgess' square neighbors: Joan Luchetti-Elam, who had just retired from working as a school nutritionist the previous Friday and her husband Timothy Elam, a licensed social worker who worked on weekends as a train conductor.

Mrs. Elam testified that David was "about the best neighbor I've ever had. And I've lived in a lot of nice areas in Reno all my life, and David is the nicest neighbor that I've ever had. He's the kindest, most gentle man that you ever want to meet."

Mrs. Elam testified that she knew he was a Hells Angel who owned a whorehouse but that, "David is invited in our home. He's family to us. And he's always in and out of our home. We have parties, garden parties that David and I put on together for our neighbors, for all the neighbors to come. We put a sign out front that anyone in town can come, and we have sometimes a hundred people show up."

"Does David have an interest in photography?"

"He does. He takes all kinds of pictures of my garden, and at our garden party he puts on a slide show."

"And have you ever gone to David's home?"

"Yes. He has a pool, and all summer my children and my grandchildren and myself swim there, and he allows…he has an open door policy at his house, and all the neighbors are allowed to swim there if they want as long as there's an adult supervisor. We can go there even when David isn't home. He allows people to come and use his, his pool and…."

"Then, how do you get into his house? Do you need a key?"

"It's totally open. His front door doesn't lock. I think it's broken. And, you know, so he has people in and out a lot of times." Then Barrett invited Mrs. Elam to say, "Well, I know that he's home all the time. I can tell you that. He…I think I go out more than he does, and I'm 70 years old, so I don't go out very often.. And he's home all the time, all the time. I mean, he…you know, unless he goes to one of his meetings, then he comes home. He does not go out. He stays home and gardens and does his computer and watches TV. He's a very kind. gentle man."

Unfortunately, in hindsight, it might not have been wise of Barrett to ask a defense witness to portray a defendant accused of being obsessed with child porn as a guy who stays home and stares at his computer all the time.

When her husband Timothy testified, he described "David as perhaps his own worst enemy. He is somewhat of a rugged individualist, and I think a lot of this is out of choice. He has a strong need to make a statement, and he does. And this is the wrong type of statement. I'm sure he wishes that this had never taken place, and certainly I wish that for him also." Timothy Elam's statement reflected the fact that he had been led to believe by Barrett that Burgess was guilty of possessing child porn.

Barrett showed Elam some of the captioned photos of Rachael Curtis and asked him, "Based upon, what, your ten years of association with Mr. Burgess and your observations of him with children, do you have an opinion as to whether or not he's the sort of individual to take the kinds of pictures you see there and to write the sort of things that you've read to yourself?

Elam replied, "I do have an opinion."

"What is that?"

"I have an opinion that I would assume that some of these pictures or these pictures were taken by David but I can't imagine David ever writing this kind of literature or thinking this type of...these types of thoughts...knowing...knowing David."

When Anderson cross examined Timothy Elam he began a recurring theme in the trial. "And again. you don't know what that man does in the privacy of his home, do you?"

"I do not."

"And you don't know what he puts on his computer in the privacy of his home, do you? Just a yes or no, sir."

"I do not."

Russell Schmitt, Elvin Ehrhardt and Randall Huff all testified that they observed the highest professional standards when handling the evidence against Burgess. Barrett never questioned the chain of custody of the evidence. And, for the rest of the first day of the trial Agent Scott Hughes told the jury that the Maxtor was 120 gigabytes big and he explained the difference between a folder and file.

Hughes told the jury that Burgess had a website. "Just out of curiosity," Anderson asked the agent, "during the course of your investigation of this matter did Dave...*davesworld81* ever come up in the course of this investigation?"

"Yes, it has."

"And what is *davesworld81*?"

"It's a website," Hughes replied, "that Mr. Burgess maintains about his, about his life."

*****

The second day of the trial began with a discussion between Judge Johnson, Prosecutor Anderson and Barrett the public defender about what additional pornography Anderson would be allowed to show the jury. There was no actual, physical evidence to connect any of this to Dave Burgess except the chain of custody of the evidence sworn to by the police. Anderson particularly wanted to show the jury "text documents" he claimed Burgess had written.

"What distinguishes the text documents in this particular case," Anderson told the judge, "is the fact that the text documents, the three that I'm offering, all relate to Rachael and Uncle Dave. You'll hear testimony today from an FBI agent from Reno that Rachael Curtis, who is the young girl whose picture I showed to the witness yesterday, Mr. Elam...."

"The latchkey kid," the judge asked.

"The latchkey kid, spends hundreds, you know, spends lots of time, hundreds of hours, hundreds of times she's been seen with the defendant. She calls the defendant Uncle Dave. And if you look at these stories that we've cited or that we've included, they relate to Rachael and Uncle Dave. And they relate to sexual abuse of Rachael and that sort of thing. The images that we have culled out, and boy, our 100...the 700 series were nothing more than compilations of photographs that the defendant had put together on Rachael that I think if not pornographic were pretty close to, pretty close to it. But they certainly were lewd and lascivious, particularly when you coupled them with the text. But suffice that to say we believe that if you look at the text documents, you couple those with the Rachael pictures that we still are gonna be able to produce, they go a long ways towards establishing identity and use of the computer by the defendant. We think obviously these are...to say that they're salacious is

119

an understatement. And I... even with, like the first one we would be willing to limit even that one to just the first two and a half pages, because in those two and a half pages the name David, the name Rachael occurs again and again.

"The next story, Judge...and that first story, by the way, I am citing to, is entitled Tami...Tami.doc. The next document, 601, is entitled OnMyLap.doc. And once again it's Rachael and Dave, and the text refers to sexual abuse being perpetrated on Rachael by Dave. And we believe, once again, that is very indicative of identity in this particular case. We, once again, would be more than happy to even...and remember, Judge, that when we first started talking about this process, we had of these types of text documents all relating to the defendant. All relating to Rachael and Dave, and, or Dave and other children. And, I'll get to the other children in just a moment. But suffice it to say, again, we'd be more than happy to cull out and even reduce this document to one or two pages. Again, simply to show the jury that the defendant has these Word documents relating to him and another...to this girl that's so frequently seen at his house or at least a girl with that same name.

"The next document...if you look back at our 300 series, there are a series of photographs of young boys that appear to be just preadolescent."

"Where are we now," the judge wanted to know. Part of Anderson's prosecutorial style is to incessantly create a cloud of confusion that obscures reason. The fact was that there was nothing to link the stories Anderson wanted to show the jury except the integrity of the chain of custody of the evidence – which is to say the words of policemen.

"I'm sorry, Judge," Anderson babbled on, excitedly and all in such a rush that the court reporter didn't bother to punctuate most of it. Exhibit, "Six-oh-two. And this document is entitled "Rachael6.doc."

"And this story talks about Rachael and some boys being involved in sexual activity, talks...the narrator talks about taking photographs of the boys, and then the next thing you know a girl by the name of Rachael shows up. And...and all of these preadolescent children engage in sexual activity. Well. we have in the 300 series a series of photographs of boys involved in group sex that were found on the defendant's computer. We think that that links up with those photographs. Once again. we believe the document speaks to the identity and to the person who is under control of that hard drive."

Anderson's hysterically fractured syntax aside, he was probably exactly right. For more than a month before the smut was discovered, Burgess' computer equipment was under the control of the smut police in Wyoming. If nothing else, the pornography Anderson wanted to show the jury illustrates the extremes to which someone went to frame Dave Burgess. If Anderson was to be believed, someone had created 15 text documents intended to portray Dave Burgess as a sexual pervert.

"The final document is probably most interesting because it again talks about Rachael. It again talks about David, and the topic of conversation of the story focuses in on David and Rachael being involved in sexual activity. But more importantly it also talks about David being fascinated with and utilizing Rachael's panties for purposes of sexual enhancement and enjoyment, which just was a huge theme that we saw throughout all of these photographs that we saw on the defendant's photographs...on the defendant's computer in a lot of the text messages...or a lot of the images that he took of Rachael he would insert comments about her panties; about utilizing her panties for sexual enjoyment and that sort of thing. So, again, we believe that it's a document offered not for the...not for anything other than it goes to identity and it identifies the defendant as the person under...who has this Maxtor under his control.

"Again, we...if the Court...and, again, we started with I think 15 stories. We've culled that down to four. And, we would even be willing to take out all but the first two or three pages of these stories, Judge, at the Court's direction and discretion. But we do believe that the stories do go to identity.

"Now, I understand that we're playing...that the courts have held these text documents should be handled very carefully by the Court because of their prejudicial impact. We do not want, by any stretch of the imagination, to unfairly prejudice the defendant. And, we are not offering these just to show propensity. If these did not have the references to Rachael and Dave, we wouldn't be offering them, quite frankly. But it's the references and the continual discussion of Dave and Rachael that we believe are so important and so highly relevant in this particular case. Again, to show the identity of the individual who had that hard drive under his control."

Barrett objected, as any layman would have. What was interesting about Barrett's objection is that he assumed, as Judge Johnson assumed, that Burgess had actually carried his child pornography collection around with him on his travels. "Same objection. Same problems. If it's offered for identity, there are other less prejudicial ways to do it. Such as, the Government has in its possession, and un-objected to, photographs of this defendant from the hard drive. Or at least that's what they say. It's a picture. Here's the guy. Here's his face on the hard drive. You can't get better identity than that. Why do you need...why do you need these writings other than the rationalization that it's for identity? Not only that there's no evidence, other than the assumption being made, that Mr. Burgess wrote the documents. That assumption is based upon reference to a fella named...a person named Dave and another person named Rachael who coincidentally or intentionally maybe are included in the writings by someone. But the assumption being made that it was Mr. Burgess who wrote it is simply wrong.

"All of the other information that the Government provides us; the Government's fascination with panties apparently, that...you know, fascinating or otherwise to Mr. Burgess or the Government during this case, it's not, it's not information that's charged. It's not unlawful. Talking dirty and liking panties isn't a crime. So to what purpose is that...are those items presented?"

In the end, Judge Johnson let Barrett win one.

*****

Agent Scott Hughes returned to the stand to complete his testimony on the second day of the trial. He explained that it was by pure luck that he happened to examine the Maxtor hard drive first. "The three items of evidence were in our evidence locker located at our ICAC office. I...the first item of evidence I happened to pull out, of the three that were stacked together, was the Maxtor hard drive. There was no cables with that, so in our laboratory or evidence locker slash lab there's a workbench in there. I was able to disassemble that item of evidence and pull the actual hard drive out of it and then started the process of the examination.

Neither Anderson nor Barrett asked Hughes about the expired search warrant, his meeting with the Assistant Attorney

General or the go-ahead from the paralegal. Instead Hughes explained: "The scope, or the umbrella, of which that first search warrant was written by Special Agent Schmitt did not include images of child pornography. And, therefore, once I observed those, I stopped. And on the afternoon of September 6th I prepared a warrant for those three items, and then I received that warrant, it was signed by a local judge here, and continued the search for those types of images of child pornography."

Hughes also found files, including deleted files, from *davesworld81*, which would make perfect sense if the Maxtor was the broken drive Burgess and Byars had used to back up Burgess website before replacing it with another Maxtor.

Anderson had Hughes take the jury through a guided tour of the pornographic library in order to explain to the jury the file structure on the drive. Anderson asked, "In regards to the Maxtor hard drive, we've got an idea now of the file structure; is that correct?" And after Hughes agreed he asked, "Tell me this. The file structure that you have described here, was that in any way out of the ordinary or unusual as far as your experience goes in conducting forensic, forensic exams of hard drives?"

"It's very well organized."

"Is that what was unusual about it?"

"That…in our investigations, oft times it's not unusual to see those types of structures within the hard drives containing child pornography. Oft times they're out…they're labeled out by age, name, type of activity. Uh. That's common, but to most people…in the world of child pornography, but in the world normal, probably not."

"In other words, you don't see that degree of organization?"

"No."

But whether the porn library was well organized or not, it was hardly a database. It was unusual because of its size. But the folders and files were simply organized in the standard dedriform structure that everyone who uses the Windows operating system uses.

Hughes testified about the bare basics of the metadata attached to all files in the Windows operating system. Basically that metadata, which can be accessed within the operating system for any windows files – tells the date and time the file was created, the date and time it was last modified and the date and time it was last accessed. However, it is fairly simple to forge the date and time when any file was last modified or last accessed by simply resetting the system clock to any date and time and then accessing or modifying the file.

During cross examination, Barrett invited Hughes to connect the Maxtor hard drive to Burgess. "Let's talk about some fairly routine investigative techniques. For example, the serial number on the Maxtor...." "You had that?"

Hughes admitted, "It was smudged."

"But you were able to raise it?"

"No."

"You don't know what the serial number is?"

"I can see the serial number and make a well educated guess. Yon can see on the exterior it's smudged."

"Did you put in your reports that there...a serial number...."

"Yes. When I got to the inside of it, I could read the serial number off the interior."

"Alright. And so what efforts, if any, did you make to determine or to follow that serial number back to the manufacturer and ultimately to the location to where it was delivered?"

"I did make an attempt, but I was unsuccessful in finding out where it went to."

"Okay. How close did you get?"

"Not very close. To a distribution center."

"Where?"

"In Nevada."

"Nevada?"

"In Las Vegas, Nevada."

"Okay. And you don't know where it went from there?"

"No, sir."

"Okay. How about the Seagate hard drive?"

"The same with it, also."

When Hughes left the stand, the jury had been flogged with "just loads" of child pornography, but there had been no testimony that Burgess had put the files on the drive. Nothing Hughes said proved or even suggested that. The only proof ever offered in the trial that Burgess had put the offensive library on the hard drive was the coexistence of the child pornography on the drive with material from Burgess' site. Nothing was ever offered to disprove the possibility that the pornography was loaded on the drive after all the site backups had been loaded onto the drive.

"In other words, if I had a batch of files all of different dates, different times, different...all the information you've talked about, and it was a series of files either on a disk or on another computer, I can transfer all of those files intact to a hard drive, couldn't I," Barrett asked.

"As well as part of those files, yes."

"Sure. So I take one computer and I transfer all of these random access dates and creation dates, and I can do that to another computer or to a hard drive?"

"Yes, sir."

"Intact? It doesn't change the dates, the access times, the creation dates, or anything like that, does it?"

"To my knowledge, no," Hughes said. None of the pornographic files were encrypted.

Anderson then called a witness who testified that child pornography is not a victimless crime. She was Ann Pancoast, the indispensible and "hard to book" FBI Agent for whose appearance the trial could not be delayed. Pancoast had first seen one series of photos in October 2000. They showed a ten year old child being abused in Jefferson County, Missouri. No one asked Pancoast how the photos got on the Maxtor hard drive. The images were, however, part of the library of images stored in the Cheyenne ICAC porn collection.

The next witness was Reno based FBI Agent Edward Duffer and in direct examination Anderson stumbled into another revelation that illustrated how ill prepared Barrett was to defend Burgess. Duffer had visited the motel room in Winnemucca, Nevada where the nude and semi-nude photos of Rachael Curtis had been taken. It wasn't that hard to establish because the room number was in one of the photos. The photos were taken during a biker rally called "The Run-A-Mucca in Winnemucca." Anderson showed Duffer a photo after establishing who Duffer was and where he worked

"Ah. very good," Anderson said. "Who are the individuals in that picture? "

"Starting from the right to left, the young female is Rachael Curtis. The man in the middle is David Burgess. And actually the person on the left, the face is a picture of an unknown female that is in one of the...it's in the office at the residence of David Burgess. It's a picture of a female on his wall in his office at his residence in Reno, Nevada."

In cross examination Barrett asked, "You identify Rachael Curtis although you've never met?"

"That is correct."

"How do you know Rachael Curtis then?"

"I've done enough investigation to know who she is."

"What do you mean? Enough investigation of what?"

"I can explain."

"Sure."

"Um, for instance, I actually reviewed an interview where she was…a tape where she was interviewed. She looks exactly like those photographs in that particular interview."

"Okay. Stop just a moment," Barrett said.

"Yes, sir."

"You did an interview?"

"I did not."

"Oh, you observed a taped interview?"

"Correct."

"And Rachael was in that taped interview?"

"And she identified herself as Rachael Curtis."

Two days into the trial, it was all news to Barrett. "This was a videotape?"

"Correct."

"And where did the interview take place?"

"At the Reno Police Department in Reno, Nevada."

"Who conducted the interview?"

"Detectives of the Reno Police Department."

"One or more?"

"One. "

"And who…there was just Miss…a person identified as Rachael Curtis on the video and one detective. Is this a male or female?"

"This was a male."

"How long did the interview last?"

"I'm not sure. Probably approximately about hour and a half maybe."

The video recorded interview actually lasted 29 minutes and it took place on October 25, 2007, the day of the FBI Swat raid on Burgess home. After the interview, Rachael stayed in the interview room until a friend arrived to take her back home. The full length of the tape is one hour and 57 minutes, which indicated the entire time she was kept in the room. Most of that time she was alone.

During the interview the young girl said she called Burgess "Uncle David" because she was close to him. She said she had stayed at his home for as long as several days and sometimes she used his address as hers. The girl also told police that Dave Burgess had never touched her inappropriately or showed her pictures of sex. The police then showed this 14 year old child copies of the photographs someone had obscenely captioned. The photos the police made her examine included the doctored photograph of a grown woman with Rachael's head mounting a man. Rachael said, "he takes pictures, but not like that." She became visibly upset and complained that Burgess had never "seen her naked." She said she did not know "where that stuff is coming from." She insisted the text on the photos "wasn't true." After reading one caption she said Burgess "has never said anything like that to me in my life."

Anderson told the judge he had had no idea the video interview existed until the night before but that now that it had been discovered under cross examination he would be delighted to share it with the defense. Anderson said it didn't think he had had an obligation to share the tape with Barrett "because the charge here is the possession of child pornography and the transportation of child pornography. And, quite frankly, that may, in fact, have bearing on a production charge somewhere else, but it does not have bearing on whether or not the defendant possessed and transported child pornography." This was after Barrett had made the jury look at the photos of Rachael. Then he added, "I'd also note that Rachael Curtis is here in Cheyenne. She's been subpoenaed to appear before this Court by the defense, and the defense has interviewed her. I also think that that ought to be considered." Actually Barrett hadn't interviewed her. His investigator had, for a total of about ten minutes.

With that, the prosecution rested and, as is typical in major cases, Barrett moved for a directed "judgment of acquittal, your Honor. And I would do so on the grounds and for the reasons that I believe it's abundantly clear that the Government has failed to carry its burden...although the burden is somewhat slighter at the close of their case in chief...they've failed to carry their burden in this matter by proof by a preponderance, other than the fact...by either a preponderance or a *prima facie* case, aside from the fact that Mr. Burgess' image appears amongst others. There is no evidence of his knowledge…there is no evidence of his intent, and there is no evidence except highly circumstantial evidence of that fact of his possession and control of the Maxtor hard drive in this case."

Johnson denied the motion because at the time of the traffic stop, Burgess had taken the blame for the entire pack's drug stash. Burgess had told Arnell that everything in the Freightliner "is mine."

Judge Johnson said: "The evidence in this matter is circumstantial. Which, is entirely appropriate, to establish a *prima facie* case by a preponderance, as summarized by Special Agent Hughes. That is, the admissions that were made by the…that are alleged to have been made by the defendant at the time of his arrest near Evanston, Wyoming, the location and circumstances of finding the item, the Maxtor hard drive, within and secreted under…within the motor home and the circumstances of that, the forensic examination revealing personal photographs, personal documents, newspaper articles featuring the defendant, and images of trips and events in the defendant's life would all I think be sufficient to allow this matter to proceed. The Court will deny the motion at this time and will call the jury back in, and we'll excuse them until…how are we looking for tomorrow?"

*****

The third day of the trial began with a discussion of more evidence Barrett had never seen. It was the FBI analysis of the forensic search of all the computer and photographic equipment seized during the Swat raid of Burgess' home in October. It was called "A Computer Analysis Response Team Report of Examination"

Anderson interrupted to set the record straight. "May I respond, Judge? Your Honor, the reports that Mr. Barrett references were first seen by the U.S. Attorney's Office or the Wyoming ICAC team yesterday afternoon about 5 o'clock. Now, I don't use that as an excuse, Judge. We were told by the FBI office in Reno, first, in regards to the interview of the young lady, potential witness in this case, that she had in fact been interviewed, and we were aware of that for a long time, but the information that we received never indicated that there was a videotape, and it came as a complete surprise to us, and we only found out about it yesterday…or late Tuesday night. That would be the 15th. In regards to these…we were

128

informed that computer equipment had been seized from the defendant's home as part of a search warrant on October 25, 2007, that they had been submitted for an exam and nothing of interest was found. Then we get this CART report which obviously contains the results of it."

"We were in communication with the FBI in Reno, and we were aware that a computer had been seized and that nothing of interest was found. No child pornography. But we didn't take it the extra step. And for that standpoint it's not the agent's fault. It's my responsibility for not having followed up with that. And all I can say is, Judge, we did not do it out of a deliberate attempt to withhold or to in any way prejudice the defendant. It was simply an oversight, although it obviously...this information should have been provided earlier. I'm not going to sugarcoat anything with the Court. When we saw...when I saw the CART report last night, I recognized that it was something that had to be revealed and given over to the defense immediately, and that's where we're at today."

Judge Johnson offered Barrett a continuance. "Well, the only tool that the Court has at this point certainly is to afford the parties time to find out whether or not...what the significance of this information is."

Anderson thought a brief recess might be more like it. "What I would suggest is, and I don't know what Mr. Barrett's feeling is, is that we either take a...we take a recess for Mr. Barrett to make the calls, make the queries, discuss this over with his, his IT people, and then decide what, if any...if there's anything worth exploring in that particular area."

Barrett interrupted, "Well...."

The Judge said, "Until you see...."

But Barrett was in a hurry to get the Burgess case over and done with. "We have witnesses from out of town that are here and available."

Johnson asked, "You would like to present them?"

"I think maybe what we ought to do Judge," Barrett said. "At least get whoever we can on this morning. Mr. Jone will be in town this afternoon. I can have him review that (the FBI report) quickly."

So then Barrett finally made his opening statement to the jury. He was briefer that Anderson had been. He told the jury he was in a hurry. He said, "Good morning, ladies and gentlemen. I'm gonna be brief because I think we want to get on with this thing as much as we can. It's been a kind of stop-and-go situation here.

"The Government's rested. They've put on their evidence. We've cross-examined. I told you early on that that cross-examination is part of our case. Now here is the rest of it. And in general what are you gonna hear? You're gonna hear from people, Hells Angels members, people who know Mr. Burgess. You're gonna hear about him. You're gonna hear that the Angels have rules and that those rules are, to put it euphemistically, strict with regard to treatment of individuals and in particular children. You're gonna hear about access to Mr. Burgess's home and not because there may or may not have been some other dude did it, who knows, but because Mr. Burgess, a sophisticated computer individual, is a guy who allows access to his home, to his refrigerator, to his books, to his computers, to his property generally, and he allows it without restriction. So you're gonna have to make a decision in the end that I'll argue in closing arguments. You're also gonna hear from people if you recall, the Winner Motel and the Winnemucca...the Run-A-Mucca, to Run-A-Mucca at Winnemucca and the pictures that were taken there and the accusations against Mr. Burgess and the implication that he was here alone with these girls and these children. Well, you're gonna hear from the adults that were there and the girls that were there. What you're gonna hear is he was never alone with them, never took a photograph, and I believe at the end of that you're gonna believe them. And you're gonna believe them not just because they say it but because the Government's exhibits themselves indicate that when one of these photos was taken Rachael Curtis wasn't alone in that room. That's the Government's evidence. So I asked you in the beginning and I ask you now. We want to get on with this. We want to put our evidence on. We want to complete this. We want to get this case to you. So keep an open mind. The pictures you've seen, the images you've seen, and the images you'll probably see again make you angry. They're horrible. They're just heartrending to see that sort of thing. But keep an open mind. Listen to this evidence as well, and wait for all of it to come in. Thank you."

That was it.

The first witness Barrett called was Troy Regas. After reminding the jury that Burgess' first character witness was a Hells Angel, Barrett continued his argument with Regas about his putative defense: "Cops in Reno are bad, but the cops in Wyoming are good."

"Alright," Barrett began. "By the way, how are you treated by law enforcement officers out here? In Wyoming?"

"Objection. Irrelevant."

"Sustained."

Barrett continued to needle Regas. "Are you treated well by...have you been treated well by the people of Wyoming?"

"Objection irrelevant."

"Sustained."

But Barrett wouldn't stop. "Since you've been here no one has treated you badly, have they?"

Maybe Troy Regas thought if he just answered the fool he would go back to the case. Troy managed to say "Absolute..." before Anderson objected again.

"Objection irrelevant."

"Was the answer no," Barrett asked.

"Absolutely not. They haven't treated me bad at all."

"Good." Barrett enjoyed some victory in his head.

"It's still irrelevant, ladies and gentlemen," Judge Johnson told the jury.

Barrett grumbled, "Struggle to get a compliment."

In an excruciatingly slow and unfocused direct examination, Barrett got Troy Regas to admit he had been convicted of a felony, that Burgess' home was never locked and that Burgess never restricted access to any of his computers or any of his DVDs or CDs, before returning to the subject of the Hells Angels. "With regard to the Hells Angels club and your chapter, well, not even your chapter, you have rules, you have regulations governing the conduct of its members?"

"Yes, we do."

"Are you familiar with those rules?"

"Very familiar.

"How...how are you familiar with them?"

"Um, I'm a...I participate, uh, very thoroughly with the Hells Angel Motorcycle Club in every aspect."

"And so are you familiar with and conversant with the rules and regulations of your members governing the treatment or maltreatment, if you will, and abuse of children or members' children?"

"Yes."

"Alright. What are the rules?"

"The rules are if somebody did something like that, we would kick them out with extreme prejudice. It would not be tolerated in any way whatsoever."

"And I assume even more so if a member's child were involved."

"Absolutely."

"Okay. Do you know a gal by the name of Rachael Curtis?"

"Yes, I do."

"Now, have you ever seen child pornography on any of David's computers, CDs, or DVDs?"

"I never have."

"And if you had seen such items, what would you have done?"

"Uh...."

"As a member of the club?"

"I would have, uh, got together with my other members, and I would have made sure that David, uh, was no longer a part of anything to do with our club and our life and that all Hells Angel Motorcycle Club property was returned to the club and, uh, that he didn't own any of it, period, whatsoever."

"Were you aware that David's photograph appears throughout...well, not throughout, but interspersed with these items?"

"Yeah. It's a little make believe to me. I can't imagine that David would do anything like that or put his pictures with any items like that. It's ridiculous."

"And there are some pictures that include a narrative, a written portion, some of which may even say Dave. Are you aware of that?"

"Yes, I am."

"Does that in any way...you haven't seen it, of course?"

"I have not seen it."

"Okay. Would that in any way change your opinion with regard to your level of comfort in having your daughters and other children around David?"

"It would not, 'cause I know David did not do that."

In his cross examination, Anderson tried to put the Hells Angels on trial. "Just the question. Is possessing cocaine a violation of your rules?"

"It's not in our rules."

"So that wouldn't be a violation?"

"Uh. no."

"Is that the answer?"

"No, it would not."

"So it's okay to possess narcotics."

"No, it's not."

"Well, I'm just by your rules."

"Not by my rules."

"But by the club rules. Now, in regards to the club, you mentioned that somebody that would abuse children would be kicked out with, quote, extreme prejudice, unquote. Correct?"

"Yes."

"So somebody that might possess child pornography that was also a member of the Hells Angels might not want to advertise that fact. Would that be a fair statement?"

"Sure."

"They'd want to keep it secret, wouldn't they?"

"I would think so."

Then Anderson decided it was time to rub the ferocious Hells Angel's nose in the obscenely captioned photos of a little girl all those Angels were honor bound to protect. "Alright. You've got a big book in front of you, Mr...is it Vegas?"

"Regas."

"Regas. Excuse me."

"R-e-g-a-s, Regas."

After making fun of his name and after making Troy Regas look at photo after photo of little children having sex with sausages, Anderson said, "Okay. That's good enough. Those first few pages that you looked at, do you agree that that's child pornography?"

"Very disgusting, yes."

"Now, in regards to Mr. Burgess and your relationship with him, you told us that you know how he interacts with children."

"Yes, I do."

"You've seen him interact with children?"

"Yes, I have."

"Have you ever heard him referred to as Uncle David by any children?"

"In our motorcycle club we're all uncles. I have about…you know, we're all considered uncle. I'm Uncle Troy. He's Uncle David. And we have lots of nieces and nephews all over the world. And that's how we refer to each other. We're brothers."

Then Anderson made Regas look at photos of Rachael. "Do you see that picture?"

"I do now, yes."

"And do you see the text that's on that picture?"

"Uh, the picture itself, yes, I do."

"And there's text on it, isn't there?"

"Yes."

"And what does that text say?"

"It says, 'Look, Uncle David, I have a big girl pus now."

"Do you think that that might be pronounced another way, too?"

"I'm sure it is. That's how it's spelled. And I know David didn't do that."

"Well, I understand that. Did you do it?"

"Absolutely not."

"So you don't know what Mr. Burgess does when he's alone in private, do you?"

"I know a lot of things about David and I know he'd never do this."

Troy Regas was a tough witness for Anderson to crack. "I understand that, and I don't want to argue with you…."

"I don't either."

"…please, sir. If you'll just listen to the questions I put to you and try to answer them, this will go a lot easier. Okay?"

"Sure."

Anderson began a line of questioning about Rachael and how she became a virtual ward of the Nevada Nomads charter of the Hells Angels Motorcycle Club."

"Her natural mother is a bad person."

Anderson showed Regas more porn. "And who is that a picture of?"

"That is, uh, uh, Rachael."

"Do you see that picture?"

"Yes, I do."

"And who is that a picture of?"

134

"It's David Burgess and, uh, Rachelle."

"It's pronounced Rachelle?"

"No."

"…or Rachael?"

"Rachael."

On and on Anderson continued, showing Troy Regas – and also the jury – photo after photo. Speculating that a collage must have been assembled by Burgess because of Dave's amazing computer skills. Asking him about the Winnemucca Run-A-Mucca. Making him say out loud:

"Uncle Dave's Pussy Meat Princess."

"Now, would making a picture like that result in a termination of a member's membership with, as you said, extreme prejudice?"

"Yes, it would."

"Okay."

"He did not make this picture."

"Pardon me?"

"He didn't make this picture."

On and on Anderson delighted in making Regas look at child porn – photo after photo after photo. Barrett never objected.

"Again, we're taking a picture…do you know who that picture…that is, who is depicted?"

"Yes."

"…in that picture?"

"Yes."

"And who is that?"

"Rachelle. I mean, Rachael."

"And would taking a picture like that result in a member's termination with extreme prejudice?"

"Yes they would be terminated from our charter."

"In regards to these photographs that I just showed you, 854, what was it, 816 as I recall, 834, do you know who took those pictures?"

"Uh, I believe some little girls did."

"Tell me about that."

"I've just heard that some little girls were together in a room and they took pictures of themselves."

"Alright. With whose camera?"

"Uh, I don't know that."

"So let's hear this, this story. I'll ask for the hearsay. What's the story?"

"That's all I know."

"Ah. Who put the text on it?"

"Uh, I don't know who put the text on it, but, uh, someone who was very jealous."

"Jealous of whom?"

"David."

"So what we have here is, is something that's motivated by jealousy? Now, who would that be?"

"You would have to…."

"Would that be you?"

"Absolutely not."

Then Anderson did what he did with all the character witnesses. "You don't know what the defendant does in his private time, do you?"

"I know a lot about what David does, and I know he wouldn't do this."

"Well, thank you very much, and I appreciate your opinion, but the question to you was this: You don't know what
Mr. Burgess does in his private time, do you?"

"Not all the time, no."

"Thank you."

*****

Sohn Regas answered the same set of twenty questions Barrett asked every defense witness. Dave Burgess liked to take photographs and work on his web site. He never locked his house. He was generous and practically everyone was welcome in his home. He was kind to children and no one ever saw him do or say anything inappropriate to a child. Sohn testified that if any of the Nevada Nomads was suspected of child abuse "we would kick him out for conduct unbecoming and send him down the road."

Barrett asked, "We have some photographs in evidence here that show David with his arm around some gal at a bar. Is it uncommon for, for lack of a better term, and it's my term, is it uncommon for civilians to want to have their picture taken with a Hells Angel?"

"People ask me all the time."

"Okay. So it's not unusual for a member to be asked to have his picture taken with a …with men, women, and children?"

136

"I don't do it a lot of time. People ask me to. If I do, I usually only do a facial shot."

On cross examination Anderson wanted to know, "Just out of curiosity, why only a facial shot?"

"Because to me it's like selling the patch."

"Now, if a fella had cocaine in his possession, would that be a violation of the rules?"

"No, it would not."

"So possessing narcotics is okay?"

"It's not against our rules, no."

"Yeah. And, let's see, get convicted of aggravated assault, beating up some other member of some other club, that wouldn't be against the rules?"

"No, it's...."

"Like kind of elevates you in the eyes of your fellow members?"

"It could deval...you know, you could go down as well."

"Yeah, if you got beat up."

"No. No if...if it was wrong."

"How is it viewed on one club member testifying against another club member?"

"Uh, it's not done."

"It's not done, is it?"

"Yes."

"Yeah. You wouldn't want to see Mr. Burgess...your former brother in law...."

"Still kind of current brother in law, but yeah."

"Still kind of current?"

"They're separated, but still married."

*****

The next witness was Misty Beckman, an absolutely stunning blonde who was Dave Burgess live in girlfriend for more than a decade. When Barrett asked her if she had any children she began to weep. Barrett hadn't prepared her either, "Yeah, wait for the tough questions." After Misty regained her composure Barrett asked, "How do you know David?"

"He's my boyfriend of 13 years. We split up about a year ago."

"Okay. How did you meet David?"

"Um, his wife introduced us."

137

"Alright. He and his wife have been separated for a long time, haven't they?"

"Yes. I didn't understand that at the time, but I was later...found that out."

"Well, for whatever reason, yeah, you didn't know he was married at the time, I take it."

"I knew he was married, and I informed her and him that I wouldn't date him."

"Alright So you moved in with David?"

"Yes, after finding out their situation...."

"Okay."

"...and becoming comfortable with it."

"Okay. Explain that situation, as you understood it."

"As I understood it at the time, David and Ingrid remained married because they have taken vows till death do us part, but they certainly don't get along."

"During the period of time you lived with David were you able to observe and tell whether he had computers in his home?"

"Yes. David is a mouse potato. I guess that's what they call them."

"A mouse potato?"

"Yes. A couch potato, but a mouse potato."

"Sure. He's on the computer a lot?"

"Yes he is."

"Does he have a particular interest or hobby?"

"Yes. He has a website."

"Okay. Does he...is he a photographer as well?"

"That's true, he is. He's actually a fabulous photographer."

Burgess never restricted her access to any of his computers. He never displayed a sexual interest in children. She could use any of his computers whenever she wanted. "David let me use his computer if I ever felt like checking e-mail, because he established an e-mail box for me so that my mom could send me pictures and send me recipes and, um and send me, you know, pictures of the family and things that I was missing in Washington." David never locked his doors, as a matter of some principle or another.

"That's alright. I want to show you what's in evidence as Government Exhibit No. 118 and ask you to examine that, please. Have you seen that before, or do you believe you have?"

138

"This is my computer. May I keep it, please?"

"For a minute, okay? Hang on to it. That's your computer?"

"Yes."

"As a matter of fact, your name is on that as one of the users, isn't it?"

"Myself and David. He bought it for me." The computer wasn't password protected. It had two Windows user accounts – David and Misty.

"Do you know where that...well, let's see," the inarticulate Barrett continued. "It was found in a motor home on July 24th...."

"That is correct," Misty answered eagerly, trying to help out the defense lawyer.

"...2007."

"That's what I was told."

" Okay. How did it first come into Mr. Burgess' possession?"

"I broke the DVD player."

"When?"

"Right after my birthday that year. March 23rd is my birthday, so right after that, and I asked him if he'd fix it."

"Okay. Just a moment. So that would be right after March 23rd of 2007, is that right?"

"Correct."

"Okay."

"Correct."

"Go ahead."

"I asked him if he would fix it, because I tried to and I couldn't do it. And so finally I brought it over to his house one night, and I left it there at his house."

"Alright. And he had it in his possession then from March until it was taken in July of 2007?"

"I'm assuming that he had it until that time, but he had...he was the last person I left it with." Misty had never seen Burgess do anything inappropriate to a child. She never heard him betray any sexual interest in little girls. Simply going by her appearance, jurors would have to conclude that Burgess had an interest and very good taste in big girls.

"Do you know a young lady by the name of Rachael Curtis?"

"Yes."

"How do you know her?"

"Um, in some sense I've raised Rachael after school and before school since she was seven years old, with David."

"Okay. So I take it she would come into and out of your home and your life. Would that be correct?"

"She would come in when she got...when her dad was on his way to work in the morning, he would drop her off in front of the house, and she'd come in...he'd watch her walk inside. She'd come upstairs and get in bed with me. And then she...I would take her to school at a little...quarter after 7:00, 7:25 if I was going, you know, if I was late. Um, and then she'd be home after school, and she'd stay with us until Tracy came to pick her up. Tracy's her father."

"Did you ever see or hear or hear of anything...."

"Hear of anything...."

"...that caused you, hold on...that caused you any concern with regard to David's treatment of Rachael?"

"No. I would...didn't like that he let her...the kind of cereal he lets her eat, but that's about all."

"Okay."

"She'd be hyper in class."

Misty had been interviewed by the FBI. She had tried for months to get her computer back. All her family photos were on it. All her memories. She had no idea how the pornography got on the external hard drives.

For the rest of the trial Anderson seized on the turn of phrase "mouse potato."

"It's actually in the Webster's dictionary," Misty told him.

"Did he use his computer for purposes of cataloging photographs?"

"I don't understand what you mean by cataloging."

"Did he organize photographs on his machine, on his computer?"

"I don't know if he organized them. I know he downloaded, he would put them on there."

"Did you ever see photographs that he had downloaded onto his computer that he subsequently put like headers on or put text into?"

"I've seen a picture that he used as my...of some of us, two friends of mine, and one other daughter, and he used it as his web page. And it said this is, this is what I, kind of something to the effect of this is what I deal with every day."

"Okay."

"Because they were arguing."

"So you…your answer is yes, you've seen pictures that he had put text on?"

"Yes."

"And so he was capable of doing that?"

"I think so."

After Misty's testimony, Barrett told the Judge, "we're actually moving along pretty well." It was one of many references he made throughout the defense to getting the trial over quickly. Barrett had had to work on Burgess' case the previous Sunday. He had another trial scheduled to begin the following Monday. He would probably have to work Sunday to prepare for that. It is impossible not to think, that many of his decisions during the trial were made so he could take that Friday off.

Outside the presence of the jury Anderson and Barrett told Judge Johnson that they were close to agreeing on a stipulation of uncontested facts about what was and wasn't found by the FBI on the computer and photographic equipment seized in the Swat raid. Barrett promised the judge, "we're prepared to continue and perhaps wind up today with our live witnesses."

Johnson reminded Burgess that he had the right to testify. Burgess was considering testifying although Barrett had warned him that he shouldn't. And then Barrett presented more character witnesses: Burgess' sister in law Fara Rials who had known him since she was a little girl; Yvonne Regas and his wife Ingrid Burgess. They all agreed that Burgess was a fine, loved, loving and respected man who never locked his doors, who would never hurt children or sexually exploit them even though he did take many photographs, who spent a lot of time on his computer, who had a website and who was capable of the astounding magic of superimposing type over his photos when he wanted to do that. None of them thought Burgess did it.

"But you don't know what David does in the privacy of his home when he's alone, do you," Anderson asked over and over.

"Nobody knows what people do," Ingrid Burgess said.

And Anderson replied, "Exactly. Thank you."

*****

141

Rebecca Deschaies was Burgess' current girlfriend. They had met three years before at a garden party at Joan and Timothy Elam's. "He was the photographer for the garden. party. He had taken photos throughout the spring of the garden blooming and the lawn and the trees, and when summer came they had a photo shoot, fashion party, and a tea party with it."

Rebecca Deschaies knew how to ride a motorcycle. She had a daughter named Leza who was the same age as Rachael and the two girls became friends. She never knew Burgess to lock his doors. She knew he owned computers and they were always turned on. She had used his computers. Her daughter had used his computers to download photographs the girl took with cameras Burgess lent her. Rebecca Deschaies testified, "He's never limited my access to anything. I'm even allowed to use his cars when I need to." She never saw child porn. He had lent cameras to Rebecca, "my daughter, my daughter's friends, their classmates." Kids Burgess knew had used his computers all the time. "All the time. If there's kids there and he's not on the computer, they are." Rebecca Deschaies also knew how to superimpose text over a photo and she had seen "the kids put text to all their photos."

She had attended the Run-A-Mucca in Winnemucca with Burgess. They were accompanied by her daughter Leza, Rachael and a mutual friend of the two girls named Taylor Jennings.

"Did you have a room?"

"Yes."

"Did you share that room with anybody?"

"Yes, I stayed…shared it, excuse me, with the girls and with David."

"When you say the girls, could you…."

"Rachael, Leza, and Taylor."

"So you, the three girls, and David shared a room?"

"Yes. Along with many other people. Our room was right next to the vending booth, and we had the door open all the time."

"The vending booth, you mean where you were selling…."

"Yes."

"…T-shirts and other souvenirs?"

"Correct."

"So the door was open to that room?"

"Mm-hmm."

"It was near the booth, and people were in and out all the time?"

"Yeah. Our room was the closest one to the booth, so the people would use the rest room in there."

"So there was always someone in or out of that room?"

"Absolutely. Just like his house, we never had the door locked. It was open. "

They all shared the room from Thursday through Sunday. Rebecca testified she spent about 15 hours a day with Burgess. When she wasn't with Dave she was with the girls. There was never a time when Dave Burgess was alone with any of the girls. He "absolutely" never took any inappropriate photos. Rebecca Deschaies had become Rachael's legal guardian and referred to her as her "daughter." She was a woman of a certain age who wanted to relish her child rearing years. When asked if possibly Burgess had somehow taken a photo of Rachael in the shower she replied "My daughters would never allow that." The girls were never alone. "They were all three always together or with me."

On cross examination Anderson tried to tar the weekend with innuendo.

He asked, And how many beds were in the room that you folks stayed in?" "And there are the three girls?" "And the three girls are your daughter...." "And what's...hold on. What's Leza's last name? Leza...." "Deshaies. And then there's a second girl?" "And then there's Rachael Curtis. So there's three girls, correct?" "And they're sharing a bed? " "And are you and David sharing a bed?" "So two of the girls are in a bed, another girl is on the rollaway, you and David...what's the sleeping arrangement?"

"No, the three girls are in the bed, and David and I had the rollaway."

"And you folks stayed there the whole weekend?"

"Do the kids have a camera?"

"They're sharing the camera. "

"What type of camera were they sharing?"

"Um, a digital."

"Digital camera?" "Okay. And who does that digital camera belong to?" "At the end of the weekend did the kids give the digital camera back to David?"

"Probably not. They never give it back to him."

Anderson started pulling nude and seminude photographs out of his hat. "Who are the children in that photograph?"

"Taylor and Rachael." "That's in our room."

"In Winnemucca?" "During the Run-A-Mucca?" "Do you know who took that photograph?"

"Probably Leza. I couldn't say for sure, but more than likely Leza did."

"Now, um, next I'd like to show you a photograph...could you turn to the next photograph in that series, 827, please? And then to the big picture after it, please? Do you recognize that scene?"

"Um, I don't know about a scene, but...."

"Well...."

"I recognize our room." "...and my daughter...one of my daughters."

"And that's your daughter?"

"That's Rachael. I call her my daughter. I am her guardian, legal guardian."

"Have you been appointed her guardian by a court?"

"Yes, I have."

"And that's Rachael?"

"That's Rachael."

"And that...was that taken during the Run-A-Mucca?"

"Yes."

"Move for the introduction of Government Exhibit 827, your Honor." Now Anderson was ready to shove Rebecca Deschaies face in a dirty picture of her daughter.

The judge announced, "It is received."

Barrett objected, "Well, without the narrative, Judge."

But the really dirty part was the words. "Oh, I think the narrative is part and parcel of the document, Judge."

Barrett objected again. "No, because we don't know who put that narrative there. There's no evidence that Mr. Burgess had anything to do with that. The picture, fine. But all the, all the extraneous material that isn't yet proven and will never be proven, no, I'd object to that." And Barrett was right.

But as he had since from before the trial, Judge Johnson, simply assumed Burgess had put the dirty captions on the photos. So the jury assumed that, too. "Overruled!"

Anderson made Deshaies look at the doctored photos in front of strangers. "Is it on the monitor in front of you now?"

"Yes."

"And that was taken in that motel room on the Run-A-Mucca, correct?" "Now. is that something that your daughter would put on a picture like that?"

"That's something none of my daughters or anyone I know would put on there." On and on.

Anderson showed the woman nine more photos of her daughter with dirty captions. "Do you recognize the child in that picture?" "Who is that?"

"That's Rachael."

"And is that a collage of pictures?" "Let's talk about those pictures as we go around from, from the center. Do you see the large collage in the begin...in the center of that picture?" "And who is that, please?"

"That's both my daughters, Rachael and Leza."

"And do you know where that photograph was taken?"

"Winnemucca, in our room, on the run."

"And who does that depict?"

"That is Rachael and Leza also."

"How about in the lower left-hand corner?"

"That is Rachael and Taylor."

"Do you know who wrote up in the upper right hand corner, Rachael my little sex...or my little partner in borderline sex crimes?"

"No."

"Do you know who took those photographs?"

"I'm gonna assume the girls took those photographs because they look like photos they take all the time."

"Do you know if Mr. Burgess took those photographs?"

"I doubt if he did."

"But you don't know that, do you?" "Do you see that picture?" "Do you recognize that scene?"

"I recognize our room. That's the girls. Uh, I believe that's on Saturday morning when they all took their showers to get ready for the day." "Do you see a person that you recognize?"

"That's Rachael."

"Do you know who did take that picture?"

"I'm gonna guess, probably Leza."

"But you don't know that?"

145

"No, I don't know that. I was probably outside the door. I'm sure I was outside the door."

Photo after photo, for more than an hour, Anderson tried to humiliate and rattle Deshaies with obscenely captioned photos of her daughter, her step daughter and their friend. Whether the prosecutor's intentions were neurotic or purely tactical, the line of questioning had nothing to do with justice. "Now, on any of the photographs that I've shown you up to this point were you present?"

"Um, I was probably sitting right outside the bedroom door because that's where I was when the girls took their showers."

"Were you present when any of these photographs were taken in the room?"

"No, but the bedroom door was open."

"So the girls are running around naked in the bedroom with the door wide open?"

"With the door cracked open, and I'm sitting right there in a chair at a round table."

Anderson didn't care that the photos, as Troy Regas put it, proved that "some little girls were together in a room and they took pictures of themselves."

Deshaies had been in the room when some of the photos were taken. "You were in the room when this was taken?

"Yeah. I remember those pictures."

"You remember all of these pictures?"

"I remember this one right here. I was in the room."

"And who took the picture?"

"I'm gonna say Leza did."

"Who did?"

"Leza. She had the camera."

"Okay. Did she take all these other pictures?"

"I don't know. She can confirm that for you, though, herself."

"Good. Did she put the lettering on this?"

"I doubt that, no."

"Did she put the words on this?"

"No, she would not put the words on there."

On redirect examination Barrett asked Burgess' girlfriend, "Do you know if Mr. Burgess put the text on those pictures?" The key issue in the trial had become the text superimposed on the photos taken in the motel room in Winnemucca.

"No. I…I don't know if he did. Do I think he did? Absolutely not. He's very protective and very guarded with the girls, as I am. He treats them as a father or an uncle."

"Mr. Anderson said that you were assuming that Leza took the pictures."

"Because Leza has the camera with her all the time." And the girl had downloaded the photos to the laptop sitting on Burgess' kitchen counter – Misty's laptop.

Anderson began his re-cross examination by accusing the witness of lying. "What you really would like is for the jury to assume that somebody else put the text on that?" Barrett objected that the accusation was argumentative.

But the judge overruled the objection. "Overruled. It goes to bias."

"And in regards to Mr. Burgess," Anderson continued, "you don't know what he does in the privacy of the home?"

"Only when I'm there, and I'm there with him a lot."

"You don't know what he does when you're not there?"

"No."

"You don't know what he does when he is alone?"

"No one knows what we do when we're alone."

In essence, the case against Dave Burgess boiled down to that. A month after a flagrantly illegal search of Burgess' motorhome, child pornography was found on two hard drives some policemen said were seized from the Freightliner. There was no physical evidence, no serial numbers, no fingerprints, no DNA, to connect the drives to Burgess except the word of the policemen who participated in the prosecution. And, the most damning evidence found on the hard drives were obscenely captioned photos of adolescent girls Burgess knew. And, the case was framed by the prosecutor and the judge in such a way that Barrett would have to produce some tangible proof that Burgess had not created the captions.

*****

Barrett grasped at straws. "Were you aware that there's evidence that that Maxtor hard drive doesn't even hook up to any of the computers in this room," he asked Deshaies.

"No."

147

Anderson objected, "That's a misstatement of the facts."

"There is nothing…." Barrett actually stood up to the bully. "There is no cable in evidence that connects to any of the computers in this room and the Maxtor hard drive. Did you know that?"

The witness answered, "No."

"And they haven't brought it here either. Did you know that?"

"No."

"So they just want the jury to assume Mr. Burgess is guilty?"

"I believe so," Deshaies said.

Anderson objected. "Argumentative. Getting a little out of hand here, Judge."

"Ladies and gentlemen of the jury," Judge Johnson warned, "you will disregard the last comments by Counsel. Clearly improper. The government is not on trial here, nor is Counsel for the defendant. And for him to be using that 'they' is clearly out of bounds. Mr. Barrett, don't do it anymore."

A few minutes later, Anderson announced that Trooper Arnell, ever eager to say whatever was necessary could testify that he had seen the missing cables in the Freightliner but had neglected to collect them as evidence. Johnson refused to let Arnell take the stand to tell that obvious lie. In the end it didn't matter. Someone had to prove Burgess hadn't placed the captions on the photos.

Rebecca's daughter Leza, couldn't prove Burgess innocent. She could only repeat what her mother had already said. Barrett made the 15 year old girl read the captions, too. " Yeah, I've seen those, but not with that writing."

"Okay. But the pictures themselves you have seen. How do you recognize the picture?"

" 'Cause I took them."

"Okay. But you didn't do the writing?"

"Nuh-oh!"

"Okay. You didn't mean for those pictures…or did you? Did you mean for those pictures to be dirty or to be displayed to anybody?"

"No. Just pictures for us to have as we grew up."

"Do you remember what you did with the Winnemucca pictures."

"Stored them on David's computer."

"Why David's?"

" 'Cause mine didn't have the, like, couldn't…you couldn't turn them to black and white or anything like that, so I did them on David's."

Anderson asked the girl, "Were you aware that the FBI wanted to interview you?"

"No."

"Or that they had made a request to interview you?"

"Uh, I…yeah, they were…actually, they did want to interview me, but the way they treated my sister when they took her out of school, there was no way I was going."

So the task of proving Burgess' innocence fell to DVDJ G-Funk, or as he was identified at trial, Gene Jone.

*****

Barrett used Jone in the case to explain to Barrett what the FBI computer analysis report of the equipment seized from Burgess' home in the Swat raid meant. Jone was the computer tech in the Denver public defenders office. After noting in the FBI report that the only graphics program found in Burgess' hardware was Photoshop, Jone had gone to the ICAC offices that morning to try to determine if the lewd captions on the photos of Rachael were made with Photoshop or some other software.

Barrett lied in court about the extent of Jone's involvement in the case. And, Jone cooperated with his boss' lie. "And so the record is clear, you have been present during these proceedings and assisting, assisting me, haven't you?"

"Yes, sir." What Jone had actually done in the trial was assist with some PowerPoint demonstrations. The testimony Barrett elicited from his "computer forensics expert" was as dry and meandering as all the rest of his defense had been.

"Now, were you given or did you obtain and review yesterday, I guess early yesterday afternoon, a report from the Computer Analysis Response Team, report of examination of Las Vegas, Nevada?"

"Is it the CART report?"

"And the CART report we'll see in a later stipulation, but you were able to review that for us?" "And there was a meeting or a conference at I think about 1:30 in the afternoon at the U.S. Attorney's conference room with the individual

149

who conducted the forensics?" "Now, what materials were examined, just generally?"

"A bunch of computers, um...." "A bunch of computers, some storage devices like Zip disks or Jaz disks, which are basically high-capacity floppy drives, and some other optical devices." "I believe there were two computers and one laptop, from my recollection." "I was told they came from Mr. Burgess's home." "It was first made available to me at about one o'clock yesterday afternoon." "This report showed that...it says on here also of note Adobe Photoshop CS2...CS2 is the version number...was located and installed on the HP computer. And on the list the HP computer would be the first item that they, they searched."

"Okay. So it was determined then that there was a Photo...an Adobe Photoshop program on the HP computer that was removed from Mr. Burgess' home in Nevada?"

"That is correct."

And, then came the bombshell. DVDJ G-Funk had actually found proof that Burgess hadn't written the captions on the photos.

"Are you able," Barrett plodded on, "by reviewing images and entries such as those in evidence here, to determine whether or not a particular Photoshop or Photoshop type program was used to enter text in those materials?" "And did you suggest to me and were you directed to examine some of these exhibits that are in evidence here to determine whether a Photoshop program, such as that found on Mr. Burgess' computer, had been used to either alter or more particularly to enter text on any of these photos in evidence?"

"Yes, sir, I did check the hex or the zero one bits of the files." What Jone meant, and there is no telling what the jury thought he meant, was that he had begun the excruciatingly detailed process of examining the "hexadecimal data," or the data preserved on the doctored photos in the standard numerical format used by computers. It is what a computer forensics technician, if Burgess had been allowed to hire one, would have done first.

"And where did you do that?"

"I did that at the ICAC office this morning."

"Was anyone else present as you did it?"

"Uh, Special Agent Scott Hughes was there as well."

"So he was present and observed as you examined, I guess, two items in particular?" Out of what Anderson claimed

150

were 70,000 obscene images, and out of about two dozen obscenely captioned photos of Rachael Curtis, Jone had had time to examine exactly two. "Okay. First of all, what program, if any, was used to imprint the text on Exhibit 835?"

"Looking at the Exhibit from left to right on the top line," Jone began, "first item is the letters y-o-y-a which means yoya. In the digital forensic world yoya basically stands for a JPEG or image. Therefore, I can confirm that this is an image. Following that a few lines down, it does say LEAD Technologies, Inc., V or Version 1.01."

So Burgess couldn't have placed the obscene text over the images.

LEAD Technologies, a company headquartered in Charlotte, North Carolina, has never manufactured end user software. LEAD doesn't make software you can go into a store and buy. The company's software is very expensive, costing up to $9,000 per copy. LEAD makes specialized software for software developers called "software development kits" or SDKs. LEAD calls their SDKs LEADTools. LEADTool SDKs are generally used to make software that transforms, manipulates, enhances, processes and stores images – like the database of pornographic images in the Cheyenne ICAC offices. LEAD Technologies sells much of its software to government agencies who develop software for state and local governments and departments, like the Social Security Administration, or the Internet Crimes Against Children taskforces. Most of the software used for ICAC Task Forces around the country was developed by ICAC Agents Flint Waters and Robert Leazenby. Because LEADTools are not made for end users but rather for developers, images processed with any software using LEAD Technologies tool kits is imprinted with a LEADTools identifier that never goes away.

Burgess was provably innocent because the photos were undeniably captioned with software developed using a LEAD Technologies toolkit and they had to have been captioned during a very small window of time – between the Winnemucca run in May 2007 and the "discovery" of the offensive images in September. Since the development software must be registered and activated to work it would have been a matter of simple, but tedious legwork to determine whether Burgess had activated any graphics software that was developed with a LEAD SDK.

151

Cheyenne ICAC, however, did have at least one activated copy of LEADTools during the time Dave Burgess was framed. In addition to five Wyoming Agents, a Homeland Security Agent and an FBI Agent, Cheyenne ICAC employed two technology administrators funded by a grant from the federal Office of Juvenile Justice and Delinquency Prevention. Those technicians, as testified to during the trial by Agent Scott Hughes, the "discoverer" of the Burgess porn trove, were "the guys that keep our servers running, our databases up to snuff: as well as issue licenses for the various software programs that have been developed by Mr. Waters and Mr. Leazenby."

And, at that point in Hughes testimony, Anderson had bragged, "And, in fact, both Mr. Waters and Mr. Leazenby, who…that's the first time we've heard his name – they have developed systems and software utilized by law enforcement not only in the United States but in, I believe, 18 foreign countries."

Dave Burgess was framed. He did not place the obscene captions on the photos of Rachael Curtis. The captions were superimposed by custom software using tools sold by LEAD Technologies. Because LEAD Technologies jealously guards its tools, it requires its developers to purchase licenses for every application the developers distribute. Cheyenne ICAC developed enough image processing software to have two employees whose duties included issuing "licenses for the various software programs that have been developed by Mr. Waters and Mr. Leazenby." The discovery of the LEAD Technologies identifier in the photos Jone cursorily examined, opened a world of defense possibilities.

But Barrett, of course, totally missed the importance of what Jone had discovered.

"Is LEAD Technologies, Inc., the publisher, producer, relate to Adobe Photoshop?" "Is Adobe Photoshop and LEAD Technologies, are they the same?" "And does it…how does LEAD Technologies figure into your examination for purposes of the text imprint on these exhibits?

"I was looking for Adobe Photoshop on here. If Adobe Photoshop was the editor for this particular image, it would say on there, Adobe Photoshop."

"Okay. So for people like me, if Adobe Photoshop had been used to put the writing on the photos, it would have said Adobe Photoshop?"

"Yes, sir."

"And it does not say that?"

"It does not say. I looked through about a hundred pages of hex code, and it was not on there."

Burgess' defense was strangled by stupid. Barrett had no idea what LEAD Technologies made. Jone, the forensic expert, had only spent 40 minutes examining two photographs. And, until that day he had never heard of LEAD Technologies.

Anderson asked, "Do you know what version of LEAD Technologies software is currently being published and sold over the counter?" Jone didn't know because LEAD software is not sold over the counter.

Anderson's question was what Mona Lisa Vito, the unwilling witness in the good natured trial comedy *My Cousin Vinnie*, would have called "A bullshit question. Nobody could answer it!"

LEAD SDKs are downloaded by developers. "Are you familiar at all with LEAD Technologies software to use in editing digital images?"

All Jone knew was. "LEAD Technologies does a lot of work with both still images and moving images such as video."

"And isn't it true that a lot of people that develop websites use LEAD Technologies software? In fact, that's really one of its primary purposes?" Anderson was trying to imply that Burgess had used a LEAD toolkit to construct *davesworld81*. He had to know that Burgess was not a software developer so Anderson, as he did throughout the trial, was trying to mislead the jury.

The computer forensics expert witness, DVDJ G-Funk honestly answered, "I have no idea, sir. I do not know exactly what LEAD Technologies is. I just briefly know what it was by looking at their website."

"Okay. Let's talk a little more about the computers that we know about in this particular case. You testified that the computers that were seized from the defendant's house on October 25th of 2007 did not contain any software relating to LEAD Technologies; is that correct?"

"I did not say that, sir. All I said was the...what the CART report, which is right here, showed that the only imaging, digital imaging software installed was Photoshop CS2 on one of the computers."

"On one of the computers?" Anderson bullied on.

"Yes, sir."

"Now, that very...that computer could have had LEAD Technologies software installed upon it at one point in time, isn't that a possibility?"

Actually, that wasn't a possibility. There is always a trail with software using a LEAD toolkit.

The licensing agreement states, "If Licensee wishes to use an OEM who will modify the End User Software and copy it, Licensee must first obtain an OEM distribution license from LEAD or must require the OEM to obtain a license from LEAD. Duplication or redistribution of the End User Software, or any portion thereof, by the users of the End User Software, without a separate written redistribution license from LEAD, is prohibited." And, "Registration. No rights to copy or redistribute the End User Software are granted until such time as Licensee has properly registered and activated the LEAD SDK with LEAD and obtained its Deployment Files. Licensee may not deploy End User Software unless Licensee is in full compliance with all the terms and conditions of this Agreement."

It would have been possible, that day, to determine what software developed with a LEAD kit Cheyenne ICAC had distributed. Of course nobody ever looked. Of course, as in the rest of the case, Anderson had no idea what he was talking about. Neither did June Jone.

"I don't know," Jone said. "Um. I did not do the forensic report, or did not do the forensic study on this particular...."

"I understand," Anderson lied, "but that wasn't quite what the...the question was. It's a possibility, isn't it, that LEAD Technologies software could have been installed on that computer at one time and deleted or removed?"

"Oh, definitely," June Jone lied. Because actually, that wasn't possible. The "computer forensics expert" was simply wrong again.

"And in regards to this particular case, we do know that on July 24th of 2007 the defendant had computer equipment that
was seized from him?" "We do know that on July 24th of 2007 that that computer equipment contained child pornography, don't we?"

Actually, nobody knows that either. What is knowable is that more than a month later, computer equipment that arrived in the ICAC offices without identifying paperwork, but that resembled hardware allegedly seized from Burgess' "War Wagon" contained child pornography.

"Okay," Anderson ranted on. "We know that the items taken from the defendant on July 24th of 2007 contained massive volumes of child pornography, don't we?" Anderson insisted that Jone testify that the offensive images were on Burgess' hardware when it was seized. Jone, who at least had a logical mind couldn't bring himself to agree with nonsense. So a few sparks flew as Anderson continued to try to shove words into Jone's mouth. "And do you know how difficult LEAD Technologies software is to use as compared with Adobe software?"

"Um, I've told you I don't know much about LEAD Technologies, only that it is a...works with digital images."

"And certainly you don't know what computer was being used when Government Exhibit 335, that is, the picture of Rachel Curtis. was edited or had text imposed, do you?" "You don't know what computer was being used when that document was being created?"

Actually, if it was made with a derivative of LEADTools, there would be a traceable record of which computer. But June Jone answered, "I don't think anybody knows."

"Well, somebody does. The person that created it does. Correct?"

"Who is that person? I...the truth is I don't know."

"Mr. Jone, I don't want to fight with you."

At the conclusion of Jone's testimony the defense rested.

*****

Taking Barrett's advice, Burgess did not testify. Barrett and Anderson agreed about the FBI report of its examination of Burgess' computers. The stipulation was highly prejudicial to Burgess because in it Barrett told the jury that a "suspected but not confirmed image of child pornography" had been found.

Before they began their deliberations, Judge Johnson told the jury:

"Thank you. Ladies and gentlemen, there is one other matter that I need to read to you, and that is the stipulation that was entered into concerning the evidence that you have heard this morning, that is, the CART report. This is in the form of a stipulation of fact, and the Court will give you further instruction concerning stipulations, but among the evidence in this case that you will be considering when you retire will be, of course, the testimony of the witnesses under oath, the exhibits that I have allowed into evidence, and the stipulations that the lawyers agree to in this case.

"The United States of America, by and through its attorney, James C. Anderson, Assistant United States Attorney for the District of Wyoming, and the Defendant, David Burgess and counsel for the Defendant, James H. Barrett, hereby stipulate and agree as follows. And, by the way, this document will go into the instructions that you will receive in this matter."

"On October 25, 2007, a federal search warrant was executed at the Defendant's residence located at 2747 Mayberry drive. Reno. Nevada, by the Las Vegas Federal Bureau of Investigation and the following items were seized: One HP...and I think HP stands for Hewlett Packard...Media Center M8040N computer bearing serial number MXX716089B containing two hard drives, including a Western Digital 320 gigabyte SATA hard drive bearing serial number WMAPZ(5)7217 and a Western Digital.320 gigabyte SATA hard drive bearing serial number WMAPAS077620 [sic]. One Compaq CM1000 computer bearing serial number 334642-001 containing a Quantum 12 gigabyte hard drive bearing serial number 312814820536. One Micron Millennia Transport laptop bearing serial number 674878-0001 containing an 1 MB 2.160 gigabyte hard drive bearing serial number 46H6092E594330. A blue Motorola cell phone with camera feature bearing serial number F29GH;A2TXS. Assorted storage media including eleven DVDs, twenty-two CDs, seventeen floppy disks, one 1 gigabyte Jaz disk, one 120 megabyte superdisk, one 230 megabyte DOT optical disk, one Lexar, L-e-x-a-r, 16 megabyte compact flash memory card, one Toshiba 2.167 gigabyte hard drive bearing serial number 96K251 04, one Zip 100 megabyte disk. nine optical disks, and one Canon PowerShot A640 digital camera."

"The above items were analyzed by the Federal Bureau of Investigation Computer Analysis Response Team members in Las Vegas, Nevada between October 25. 2007 and December 21, 2007. As a result of that examination. one image of suspected but not confirmed child pornography was found on one of the seized optical disks. The Compaq CM1000 computer revealed that data had been transferred from the Compaq computer to two separate Maxtor hard drives, a Seagate hard drive, and a Firelite hard drive. The exam did not reveal the type of data transferred, the date of any transfer, or the serial number of any external hard drive to which data may have been transferred."

In his closing argument Anderson told the jury: "The testimony and the evidence in this particular matter establishes that before July 23rd or on July 23rd the defendant drove over from Utah into Wyoming. He was driving…or within his vehicle, within that vehicle, as we now know, there were the Seagate hard drive, the Maxtor hard drive, both external storage devices, and this computer. Contained on those two external storage drives a cache, thousands of images of child pornography, but; also importantly, on both of those items documents, files, linking these items directly to the defendant, personal papers, personal photographs and, importantly, text, text referring to Uncle David. That evidence, ladies and gentlemen, we submit to you on behalf of the people of the United States, the evidence that you've heard cries out for a just verdict, a just verdict being guilty of both counts. Now, ladies and gentlemen, when we started this trial, when I first talked to you I told you that, gee…the Government's got to prove elements. We don't have to prove that the defendant took any of these photographs. We don't have to prove that the defendant did anything other than the two elements that are charged in each count."

"It's uncontroverted that on July 23rd, 2007 the defendant traveled over from Utah into Wyoming. Uncontroverted. Uncontroverted that he came into the District of Wyoming. The defendant knowingly transported or caused to be transported in interstate commerce digital image files. And then we specifically named that series that Agent Pancoast investigated from Missouri. Specifically named within that Indictment are those images from Missouri. They…we know those images traveled in interstate commerce because those images were taken of that poor little girl back when she was being sexually abused in the state of Missouri. But there were a whole lot more images on that hard drive than just those, and we know that. So we know that on July 23rd, 2007 in a vehicle belonging to the defendant, on equipment found in the defendant's vehicle, a lot of child pornography was transported into this state."

"What's the key issue? Knowingly. What's the key issue? Knowingly. What's the key issue in this case? What was in the defendant's mind? Did he know that there was child pornography on this Maxtor hard drive?"

"In a case like this, direct evidence, how many individuals that would view that awful material that's contained within Government's Exhibits 300 through 335 want to be seen viewing that material, want to be seen downloading that material? Do you think that people that are interested in viewing children, innocent children, being sexually abused are gonna invite the neighbors over? Hey, Mr. Elam, hey, Mrs. Elam, come on over, we'll have a tea party, and then we'll all watch some child pornography together. People that watch and that want to catalog and that want to possess that filth, that material, they do it in private. You don't get direct evidence of people down loading, that is, somebody watching it, seeing it, doing that stuff."

Actually Cheyenne ICAC made cases by catching people in the act of downloading child pornography. That's what some of the software developed by Flint Waters and Robert Leazenby did. The software enabled agents sitting in Cheyenne to spy on sites that pedophiles used to trade kiddie porn, watched the downloads, matched the downloaded images with images in the ICAC porn bank and noted the serial numbers and locations of the downloading computers. Practically all Cheyenne ICAC did was watch perverts downloading child porn. There was no evidence that Burgess ever downloaded any of what appeared on his hard drives. In Anderson's argument, Burgess' protestations of his innocence were proof that he was guilty.

"How many people walk around with a balloon over their heads saying, gee, I know that there's child pornography on this item? Instead, what are the circumstances? Well, we know that this item, this repository, this, this bank, if you will, for data contains not only tens of thousands of well-cataloged, well-organized child pornography, it also contains thousands and thousands of references to the defendant, Mr. Burgess."

Possibly because the pornography was loaded on drives that Burgess had used to back up his website. Then Anderson made the astounding claim that unless Burgess could prove his innocence beyond any doubt, the jury should consider him guilty. Burgess could have proved his innocence and probably pointed to the exact computer in the offices of the Cheyenne ICAC Team that had been used to fabricate the evidence against him. But in this case his defender and his "computer expert" were incompetent, the prosecutor was an unprincipled bastard and the judge simply assumed Burgess was guilty.

"Reasonable doubt, ladies and gentlemen, is proof,' Anderson claimed. "Is proof that leaves you firmly convinced. It leaves you firmly convinced of the defendant's guilt, firmly convinced of the defendant's guilt. It is not absolute proof but merely proof that leaves you firmly convinced. That's what needs to guide you during the course of your deliberation. And reasonable doubt, folks, is based upon reason. Reason and common sense. Please don't go into that room and abandon your ability to reason, your ability to deduce, to deduct, and to use good old fashioned common sense. That's what's…that's why we want twelve folks serving as jurors. To use their collective common sense and reason in arriving at a verdict."

"The defendant claimed ownership. When questioned by Trooper Arnell, when questioned by Russ Schmitt, the defendant stepped up to the plate and said, yeah, I own everything in that vehicle except for a couple of the duffel bags don't belong to me. Claimed ownership of the personal property within that vehicle."

"The defendant did not dispute ownership of the computer and hard drives when given that inventory. There was the discussion about when he's gonna get those items back and why they were being taken. Why are they being taken? When are they gonna be given back? And we know that those two items contained thousands of images of children being sexually abused, thousands of images of children being sexually abused. This case isn't about, gee, what is that? We all saw those images. We all know what those images are. Those are images of child pornography."

"We know that he knows how to download digital images. We heard that testimony. We know that he had a website that
you saw, incredibly well organized. And what was one of the interesting features about it? Links to literally thousands
of pictures, links to literally thousands of pictures."

"The computer seized from the defendant's home, what do we know about that? Well, we know the Compaq, the older computer with the smaller hard drive, had been used to

159

download data to a Maxtor hard drive and to a Seagate hard drive. We know that from the stipulation. We know that he's downloaded or somebody on a computer belonging to him has downloaded material to Maxtor and Seagate hard drives."

In all, Anderson extemporaneously lectured the jury for about a half hour. Barrett winged it for about half as long.

"So what proof do they have that Mr. Burgess knew any of this material was in either this Maxtor hard drive or the Seagate? And the Seagate's not a charged...it's not in the charges, but nevertheless we keep arguing it. What evidence do they have? They have Mr. Burgess' pictures mixed in, like in this file of Mr. Anderson's, with everything else, and they say, aha, here's the culprit. It's a little more than that because of text, but I'll get to that in a minute. They stand here and they tell you here are these things. We know this doesn't...can't be operated without special equipment and that special equipment wasn't present in the motor home and so far as we know was never...none...nothing that could operate this was ever collected in Nevada. There was some evidence in the forensic examination in Nevada that similar external drives had been accessed, but we don't know where. We don't know when. We don't know why and we don't know by whom. And we don't know what was loaded. But based on that, what we want you to do is believe that because there were two Maxtor hard drives, a Seagate, and a Firelite in the home in Nevada, we want you to convict somebody, and we want you to convict him because it's just like this generally inoperable hard drive.

"So if child pornography was found in the back seat of a Chevy, and you own two Chevy's, then you'd be guilty of possession of child pornography if they could get you that way because you own something similar."

"It's almost...it's not difficult. It's mind-boggling to try and list the number of things the Government doesn't know. They don't know if the images on the Maxtor were transferred there by a computer in the possession of Mr. Burgess, but they want you to believe it was. They don't know during which periods of time those images were downloaded or loaded to the Maxtor, but they want you to believe it's Mr. Burgess because they say, look, you can't do all that at one time. Their own expert says that's not true. Remember when I asked Mr. Hughes if you could transfer entire groups of data intact and preserving the information on that data at one time?

That was virtually one of the last things I asked him about. And he said yes, you can."

"So what you have in here is a whole bunch of data and images that have access dates, creation dates. file paths, and absolutely no idea what computer they were loaded from, where they were loaded, when they were loaded, and by whom. You don't know any of that stuff: But Mr. Burgess' picture interspersed in there, so you're asked to believe that he did that. And because he did it, he knew it was child pornography. And because he knew it was child pornography, possessed it. And because of that, he's guilty. But you can't even get past the first part of it."

"Nobody's in this room saying that isn't child pornography. It is. I mean, who can watch it and not feel angry and horrified and just sad? Who can see that? But the issue isn't whether it's child pornography. The issue is whether or not Mr. Burgess knowingly possessed child pornography. The issue is whether he knew it was there."

"I've spent a lot of years dealing with people, professionally and otherwise, that I don't like, but you have to do the right thing and follow the law in spite of that. And if you really look not at the evidence but at the lack of it, nearly a total lack of it, when you return you're gonna return here and you'll find David Burgess not guilty of both counts. Thank you."

The jury began deliberating at 12:51 p.m. and returned a verdict at 4:54.

Judge Johnson said, "Would the foreman or foreperson present that to the bailiff please. All I have to do is find it here. Don't mean to keep you all in suspense. Ladies and gentlemen of the jury, you will harken unto your verdict. We. the jury, duly empanelled in the above-entitled case, do unanimously find beyond a reasonable doubt as follows: As to the charge contained in Count One of the Indictment, interstate transportation of child pornography, we unanimously find beyond a reasonable doubt the defendant, David Burgess, to be guilty. As to the charge contained in Count 2 of the Indictment, that is, possession of child pornography, we unanimously find beyond a reasonable doubt the defendant, David Burgess. to be guilty."

Barrett got his Friday off and he got paid for his "defense" of Burgess. The first thing Burgess did when he heard the verdict was to turn to Barrett and fire him. But

Barrett got his Friday off and he got paid. Then Dave Burgess was immediately taken into custody by United States Deputy Marshalls and held until his sentencing three months later.

*****

When he imposed Burgess' sentence on July 18th, Judge Johnson began by saying that Dave Burgess' apparent obsession with child pornography had been discovered to be even greater than was presented at trial.

"The defendant...at the time of trial Special Agent Scott Hughes in his investigation had examined over 1300 images of child pornography, which is punishment enough for Scott Hughes for his occupation. When he stopped the formal count and has since reviewed on one of the hard drives, external hard drives, the Seagate, which was not the primary one in this case, 31,000 additional images which he contends would meet the definition of child pornography."

"And we got a fair showing of the range of that material during the trial as images briefly were put before the jury, after being received in evidence, of the victims of this exploitation. It is a strange exploitation, in my view, in that I'm very familiar, sitting on this bench, with exploitation that is done for money in what we see by way of what is broadcast over the Internet as...I don't see a financial connection that is there. So it's puzzling in that sense. But in this case it is not a case that was discovered through the techniques that have been developed by Flint Waters but, rather, surfaced as a result of a highway patrol stop that occurred on July 24th, 19...I mean, July 24th, 2007 near Evanston, Wyoming, when Officer Matt Arnell stopped this motor home, driven by another person and occupied by the defendant. And the defendant had control over the motor home. And a search essentially drug based following a dog alert occurred. And as a result of that effort, the computer equipment was seized and ultimately found its way to Scott Hughes for a drug investigation. And upon his discovery of the first image, he sought a search warrant, and this case materialized at that point."

The judge had a few words to say about the unusualness of the apparently airtight case against Burgess.

"So this is not about something that was necessarily discovered through the use of LimeWire or Kazaa or BearWare or some other form of shareware but is a matter that came up in...through this highway stop, as I've mentioned. But whether it is, as we often see, through investigation of the Internet or through a highway stop, this conduct is not done in the public eye. It is surreptitious. Persons do it on the Internet because they feel anonymous, they feel safe, that no one will know about their dirty secret and what their activity may be either producing or passing on or distributing that sort of material of child exploitation. So it is not a great surprise to me that this defendant is not a person that possesses prior offenses in this area. He has been and felt that he would not be discovered, although the Maxtor hard drive was slid under the seat of the couch in the motor home."

"I can find no intent to distribute this material and would not pretend to characterize the evidence as indicating an intent on the defendant's part. Clearly he possessed it. And, clearly the jury found that he transported it on these computer related devices. The material in and of itself is poisonous and toxic. It horrifies jurors who are, unfortunately, required to see samplings of it. It is poisonous and toxic to the person who collects it. And, not speaking for Mr. Burgess, because he probably at this point should not be saying too much given the status of his case, but from experience that the Court has had, persons who are addicted to this, this material truly feel that they, they need help eventually with it and with their conduct."

"What we see here, although denied, and justifiably so, is an extensive collection that is...where categories of misconduct have been established and the material has been cataloged within these systems, within the hard drive. It is sizable, reflects hours of assembly – whether those materials were obtained from outside through something other than shareware or LimeWire or some computer sharing program or were acquired over the Internet. So it is extensive, it is substantial, and certainly reflects energy that was devoted to this."

Judge Johnson spoke about the kid he considered to be Dave Burgess' main victim.

"I don't know how to deal with the young person Rachael Curtis, who became part of this, unwillingly became part of this prosecution, except to note that certainly those images that exploited her, a teenage young woman, from about age 13 on to her present age, and I'm not saying that anything beyond picture taking occurred...what is in the images...but certainly the text that was attached to those images reflected great confusion and desire with regard to any parent…that was inconsistent with any parent-child sort of position. And the hundreds of pages of textual material with the first name of one character being Dave and the other the name of this individual, this young female, reflect an obsession or a, a, an…an improper interest in that regard in regard to exploiting that relationship. And that, I'll leave that there because I don't know…wish to say any more or express anything more about it."

"I do look at the other cases that have been prosecuted before this Court and really have to look in this case at the guidelines for guidance in imposing sentence in this case and will be imposing the sentence within the guideline range that has been, that has been established."

"This defendant, Mr. Burgess, has, without any, any contradiction from the Government, has done many good things in his life. He has been a Marine who honorably served his country. He apparently has helped many people and served in a philanthropic capacity in many ways in the Reno, Nevada, community, although I suspect by virtue of his position or as a licensed brothel owner that all that was not formally recognized or honored by Reno and certainly has not been here if that is the fact."

Then Judge Johnson spoke about what he considered to be the ridiculous notion that Dave Burgess might have been framed. He also made a veiled reference to Troy Regas who was convinced Burgess had been framed and had not been shy about saying it.

"I would note that an effort has been made…I'm not so sure it comes from this defendant, but appears to come from others who are close to him…that this is all a plot by the government. Absolutely no evidence of that. How a government agent…there was some testimony at trial that the door of the house was always open and I guess, presumably, government agents could sneak in and create these hard drives as a way of retaliating for the litigation that had gone on involving the Internal Revenue Service. I don't know what motive they would have. They've won most of the rounds of litigation in that regard, have collected over $2 million in back taxes and are asserting another $2 million in penalties, and all at tremendous legal expense of this defendant and those close to the brothel operation. So I…but there undoubtedly may be bad feelings that exist, but not the slightest evidence that would be credible, in my mind, to indicate that this was a setup by anybody related to the United States. I say that without, without in any way intending to minimize the fact that this defendant probably is a figure of...was a figure of interest. And certainly the indication was that Matt Arnell had received advance notice that Hells Angels were coming through Evanston, Wyoming, and were on the lookout and did see the bus or motor home at the JB's Restaurant location in Evanston, Wyoming."

Judge Johnson urged Dave Burgess to admit his obvious guilt and repent his sins.

"I would hope that at some point this defendant will be able to acknowledge his preoccupation with child pornography and the damage that it has done to his life, to his business activities, and to the family members. Certainly on July 24 traveling across...of 2007...traveling across the United States with apparently cocaine, marijuana, and a Maxtor and a Seagate hard drive and a computer containing child pornography, pretty risky behavior. And it would be very difficult to say that that could be organized by Matt Arnell with the Wyoming Highway Patrol or, frankly, anyone else with the IRS or any other federal agency."

"If it was, my guess is this was an inside job that required tremendous effort and knowledge."

Finally Johnson formally told Dave Burgess what his punishment would be and how his life would change.

"Pursuant to the Sentencing Reform Act of 1984 and those factors set forth in Title 18 United States Code Section 19 3553(a), it is and will be the Judgment and Sentence of the Court that the defendant, David Burgess, is hereby sentenced to a term of 180 months custody in the Bureau of Prisons on Count 1 and 120 months custody concurrent, to be served concurrently, on Count 2. Upon his release he will report to supervision for a 10-year period, concurrent on each count, and will report within 72 hours to the probation office in the district to which he is released under conditions, standard conditions, that he not commit any crimes, with the warning that he is required to register as a sex offender. The defendant shall abide by the standard conditions of supervised release recommended by the Sentencing Commission. He shall not purchase, possess, or use firearms, ammunition, or explosives in any manner. He shall not illegally use or possess controlled substances and will submit to random drug tests as required by law. Under the Justice For All Act he is required to submit DNA to the Bureau of Prisons and to the probation office. And he shall not...he shall make his special assessment, restitution, and fine payments and notify the probation office of any material changes in economic circumstances affecting his ability to meet monetary obligations. He shall pay all financial obligations forthwith, and those not paid immediately or through the Bureau of Prisons Inmate Financial Responsibility Program shall be paid beginning the month following his release in monthly installments of at least $200. There are a number of standard conditions related to sex offense registration. He will be required to provide state officials with any and all information required by the state sex offender registration agency, such as photograph, fingerprints."

"He shall not access the Internet with any device unless such device has filtering software and shall not conceal the names or erase the names of sites visited, and the computer shall be configured to retain history for at least 30 days. He shall not receive or send or possess images or signals or sounds, telephonic or electronically, unless part of a treatment registration...regimen. He shall not send or receive e-mails or other documents discussing pornography or sexually oriented material unless part of such a treatment program, and I can't imagine that there would be such."

"The probation officer shall have the right at any time to access any computer to search its history of sites visited and may install any hardware or software system to monitor it and may also search peripheral computer devices for images or files containing sexually explicit material. Defendant shall participate in a program of sex offender treatment approved by the probation officer as directed by the probation officer, which may include plethysmograph and polygraph testing. Defendant shall not associate with children under the age of 18 except in the presence of a responsible adult or adults who is or are aware of the nature of the defendant's background and current offense and who have been approved by the probation officer."

"He shall register with the state sex offender registration in any state where he resides, is employed, carries on a vocation, or is a student as directed by his probation officer. As an explicit condition, he will submit to a search condition related to use of a computer that relates to his person, property, house, residence, vehicle, and any computer

166

device or electronic device therein. He will participate in a program of testing and treatment for drug and alcohol abuse as directed by the probation officer until such time as he is released from it and will submit to drug and alcohol testing as may be required. He will be required to pay a one-time fee of $750 to partially defray the costs of this treatment. However...if he is...this condition is waived if he is supervised by a district other than Wyoming, which I suspect would be the case."

"Defendant shall not use or possess alcohol nor frequent establishments deriving their primary income from its sale. The Court finds that restitution is mandatory, but there has been no request for restitution, and none is ordered. The Court finds the defendant does have ability to pay a fine within the guideline range, and a fine in the amount of $20,000 is ordered. The fine is imposed concurrently on each count. There is a special assessment fee in the amount of $100 per count for a total of $200. Payments for monetary obligations are payable by cashier's check or money order to the Clerk of the District Court, 2120 Capitol Avenue, Room 2131, Cheyenne, 82001. And the defendant will participate in the Inmate Financial Responsibility Program."

"He has 10 days to file his notice of appeal from the date the Judgment and Sentence is ordered. And I find the sentence imposed is sufficient but not greater than necessary upon consideration of those factors set forth in Title 18 United States Code Section 3553."

Dion Custis represented Burgess at his sentencing. He asked, "Your Honor, before you leave the bench, can Mr. Burgess have some contact with his family before he's transferred?"

And Judge Johnson allowed, "I have. no objection to that. I'll leave it in the hands of the Marshals to supervise as they deem appropriate."

Finally, after a few brief moments of goodbyes to all that had been, and all who had been and all of what might have been, Dave Burgess was fed to a great and terrible beast. He spent six months in administrative segregation, which in some prisons is called the Security Housing Unit or SHU, at the United States Prison at Lompoc, in California. Then he was transferred to the medium security Federal Correctional

Institution at Bastrop, Texas, about 30 miles from Austin and 1800 miles from Reno.

Aftermath

Three weeks after Dave Burgess was convicted, Storey County Commissioners voted to shut down the Old Bridge Ranch. A Commissioner named Bob Kershaw said, "David has been convicted of a very serious crime, and how can we not suspend his license considering the crime he committed? It's unfortunate that this has happened from the standpoint of employees losing their jobs." The brothel closed almost immediately. "They can't conduct a brothel business at this time," Kershaw said. "Maybe there's some solution that the place can either be sold or someone else can apply for the license."

After his sentencing, the Storey County Licensing Board, which included the local Sheriff and three Commissioners, voted to revoke his brothel license but stayed the revocation for 12 months to give Burgess time to appeal. Eventually the license was revoked, and Ingrid Burgess, who had helped build the business and who ran it for more than 15 years, divorced David.

Burgess' conviction was enormously embarrassing to the Hells Angels Motorcycle Club worldwide. Most Hells Angels assumed Burgess must be guilty and wanted no part of him but Troy Regas refused to kick Burgess out of his charter. And, as long as Burgess was a member of a bonafide charter, there was nothing the club could do about it.

A reliable source with knowledge of the Hells Angels in Europe said, "The news that Dave Burgess had been charged with the kiddie porn offences had not gone down well over here. A very, very vocal section of the club wanted him kicked out straight away, innocent or guilty." The demand was made to visiting club members from the United States. Burgess charter issued a written statement to the club at large that they "considered the case to be a set up and that they would stand by Dave. "Loud outrage subsided to muttered grumbling. Only his own charter has the right to throw him out so Europe had to seethe in silence."

At one meeting with American Hells Angels an exasperated European Angel said, "Are you guys fucking stupid? We don't fucking care if he gets the chair or life for the dope, so long as you fucking well get the porn charge thrown out! You fucking morons! It's damaging the club!"

Nevertheless, Troy Regas and the rest of the Nevada Nomads stood against the world, an act of defiance against the mother club which is rumored to be dangerous.

*****

Burgess first appeal was handled by a Yale educated criminal appeals specialist named Norman R. Mueller. Mueller's 32 page appeals brief concentrated on the search that eventually led to the discovery of child porn on Dave and Misty's laptop and the two hard drives. The brief also argued that Burgess had been over sentenced.

Mueller concentrated on the traffic stop and the search of the hard drives. He did not appeal Judge Johnson's denial of a continuance on the Friday before the trial began so Burgess could get a new lawyer sufficiently informed about the case to represent him. So, because Mueller failed to include that denial of a continuance in his appeal, Burgess forever lost the right to appeal that part of his case.

The Tenth Circuit Judges who heard the appeal were particularly offended by the captioned photos of Rachael Curtis, who in all court documents in the case is referred to as "R.C."

"The images" the Appeals Court noted, "are clearly child pornography. They show a pre-pubescent girl wearing nothing but a light dress pulled up over her chest: Exhibits 805-808 show the nude child in various poses centering on her genitalia. One image shows her with an adult male." By that, the judges meant the photo in which Rachael's head had been superimposed on the body of a woman.

"These exhibits," the court continued, "include one nude image of R.C. taking a shower and several semi-nude pictures of R.C. dressed only in a towel. The images appear with graphic and vulgar superimposed text. For example, one image is R.C. sitting cross-legged on a bed wearing only a short towel (genitalia exposed) with superimposed text referring to 'Uncle David's . . . Princess.' The nude shower image contains the superimposed statement, 'I think this is one of the sexiest pictures in my collection.'"

Mueller also argued that the captioned photos of Rachael, constantly thrust in the face of every juror and every defense witness, unfairly prejudiced the jury. He thought the photos gave jurors the idea that Burgess had been molesting the girl. That is probably exactly what Anderson had in mind. But the Tenth Circuit did not care.

The prosecution's portrayal of Burgess may, the court wrote, have been "more prejudicial than probative and allowed the jury to convict Burgess, not for possession and transportation, but for other uncharged crimes." But if so, in the court's opinion, the interests of justice dictate it couldn't be helped. Fairness, the court noted, "is often a matter of perspective." Consequently, the court ruled, "the evidence was relevant and proper."

Mueller seemed convinced that the searches that led to the discovery of the child pornography were unconstitutional. In his appeal the appeals lawyer wrote, "the application of the automobile exception to search the computer and hard drives found in his motor home would grant police 'the authority to forensically analyze and conduct a general search of any computer found in any automobile which was subject to a valid search under the automobile exception.' ...because of the amount of personal information stored within," Mueller argued that a personal computer is a virtual home. In this "age of the laptop computer," he argued, such an "extraordinary expansion" of the automobile exception would "destroy a citizen's expectation of privacy in his or her computer."

"Interesting as the issue may be," the Tenth Circuit replied, "we need not now resolve it because the search of Burgess' hard drives was authorized by a warrant."

"The pertinent documents," that led to the computer search, the court conceded, "could have been more artfully prepared." The search warrant authorized the search of "computer records" that confirmed Burgess' participation in drug trafficking and Cheyenne ICAC "was only looking" for that when it found child pornography instead.

The Tenth Circuit ruled that when anything is looked for on a computer, a policeman may look at everything on the computer. If a personal computer is legally seized, as Dave Burgess' computer equipment was legally seized, nothing on it can be considered personal. "In the end," the court concluded, "there may be no practical substitute for actually looking in many (perhaps all) folders and sometimes at the documents contained within those folders, and that is true whether the search is of computer files or physical files."

The Tenth Circuit decision relied on two legal metaphors to justify the search of Burgess' computer equipment. The two metaphors that apply to computer searches are the metaphor of "plain sight" and the metaphor of the "suitcase."

The "plain sight" metaphor or doctrine says that cops do not have to be blind. If you like to keep your marijuana plants and your machine guns in plain sight in the middle of your living room, and a cop legally enters your home, either by invitation or with a search warrant, and he happens to notice those illegal things which you were foolish enough to place in plain sight, then your marijuana and your machine guns may be lawfully used as evidence to convict you of their possession.

The metaphor of the "suitcase" is more recent and specious. Simply put, it is the legal doctrine that a personal computer is not really a personal computer but only a kind of suitcase. A customs agent may open the lid of your suitcase and rummage through your belongings. If he spots drugs, guns or undeclared French perfume that evidence of your smuggling is considered to be in "plain sight" and can be used against you. The Tenth Circuit compared a personal computer to a suitcase at the border.

In its decision against Burgess, the Tenth Circuit wrote, "In discussion of reasonable expectations of privacy we likened a computer to a suitcase or briefcase because a 'personal computer is often a repository for private information the computer's owner does not intend to share with others' and since 'intimate information is commonly stored on computers, it seems natural that computers should fall into the same category as suitcases, footlockers, or other personal items that command a high degree of privacy....'

"At first blush," the judges continued, "there appears no reason to treat computers differently than, for instance, a locked briefcase in the locked trunk of an automobile. There is a privacy expectation for a briefcase or suitcase, which may contain very personal and confidential papers – particularly when well secured in the trunk of a car. Yet the automobile exception subjects the briefcase to search. So why not the computer? What is the difference between a file cabinet, suitcase or briefcase and a computer?"

But around the same time the Tenth Circuit was blowing off Burges' appeal, the more liberal Ninth Circuit Court of Appeals also considered a case involving computer searches. That case was titled *United States versus Comprehensive Drug Testing*. The case is popularly known as the BALCO case after a California business named the Bay Area Laboratory Cooperative. BALCO's most famous client was San Francisco Giants slugger Barry Bonds.

Other players who were not Barry Bonds were accused of ingesting anabolic substances only after a computer search for other records at a drug lab revealed that those other player's names were in files on a hard drive. No warrant had ever been issued to search for those players names but according to both the "plain sight" and "suitcase" metaphors anytime a computer is legally searched everything on that computer – everything – whether it is being legally searched for or not, is considered to be in "plain sight."

Two weeks after the Tenth Circuit heard the Burgess appeal, the Ninth Circuit wrote:

"If the government can't be sure whether data may be concealed, compressed, erased, or booby-trapped without carefully examining the contents of every file... then everything the government chooses to seize will, under this theory, automatically come into plain view. Since the government agents ultimately decide how much to actually take, this will create a powerful incentive for them to seize more rather than less.... Let's take everything back to the lab, have a good look around, and see what we might stumble upon."

The Ninth Circuit went on the say that "the government (must) waive reliance upon the plain view doctrine" and that computer searches should not even be carried out by police. To keep the police from doing mischief, the court ruled, legal computer searches must be conducted by "specialized personnel or an independent third party."

The Ninth Circuit ruling was not very radical. For years before the ruling, third party, so called "filter teams" have been routinely used in white collar investigations to separate what the search warrant names from everything else on a hard drive. When a banker is accused of embezzlement cops do not search his computer for evidence of that embezzlement. Third party, professional filter teams search the banker's computer to intentionally limit the search to whatever the warrant specifies. In Burgess' case, a third party would have examined Burgess equipment for evidence of drug dealing and would have been mandated by law from discovering anything else.

The Solicitor General of the United States, on behalf of the Obama Administration, appealed the decision to the full Ninth Circuit panel of judges. It was an unusual request. The Solicitor General's brief complained, "...before a search commences, case agents will need to spend days, weeks, or even months teaching both the underlying law and the specifics of the particular case to members of a filter team. These concerns will be particularly acute in cases involving national security, because spies and terrorists often receive specialized training about concealing their tracks.... In some districts, computer searches have ground to a complete halt, and, throughout the circuit, investigations have been delayed or impeded."

That Solicitor General was named Elena Kagan. When she was nominated for the Supreme Court, most public debate focused on a photograph of Kagan playing softball. Television wise men debated whether the photo indicated her sexual preference. But her opinions on personal computer searches received absolutely no public attention.

Because there was a disagreement between two circuit appeals courts, Mueller appealed the Tenth Circuit decision on Burgess to the Supreme Court of the United States on November 4th, 2009. A Supreme Court ruling would decide whether the Ninth or Tenth Circuit was correct about computer searches. The Supreme Court declined to hear Burgess' case on December 14th, 2009.

*****

Dave Burgess generally got along well in prison. He worked as a gardener. Then he got a better job working the in the Hobby-Craft tool room.

Although he despaired, he was still the same guy he had always been. He did 500 pushups and 2,000 jumping jacks a day. He kept his faith with the masculine virtues. He wrote a newsletter from prison that resembled *davesworld81* and he distributed it by email to friends who would pass it on to other friends, like *samizdat*. Like his website, the newsletter called *Dave's World Behind The Barbed Wire*, was about his life.

In March 2011 guards brought a 52 year old inmate into the cell Burgess shared with another inmate. The inmate had Stage IV colon cancer and had no control of his bodily functions. Burgess and his cell mate were expected to handle the man's disposable diapers and the inmate became another of Burgess' causes – an example of official callousness, injustice and stupidity.

The disease was messy. The new cellmate could only urinate through a catheter and he constantly bled from his rectum. The cell the three men shared was constantly soiled with blood and feces. The sick inmate was in obvious distress. Burgess began writing about the inmate and emailing friends about the man daily. "I am sorry to burden all of you we such gruesome details about my currant cell situation, but I think it is very important that this is documented at this time. I hope I do not lose my e-mail privilege for sharing this with the world, but it is what it is...."

"I have been to the Health Care Administrator and the Clinical Director to try to get a solution to this ongoing problem with no success," Burgess wrote another day. "At this point I believe I have exhausted all of my remedies here at FCI Bastrop to get my sick cell-mate the proper care he needs. I am now asking all of you, my family and friends to step in and help. First I would ask that some or better yet, all of you call and, or email the Austin *Statesman* newspaper and forward all of my news letters about my sick cellie to a reporter there."

"My main concern is for my sick cellie. He needs proper health care in an approved medical unit before he bleeds to death in our cell. Also you can contact anyone else you think may be of help."

"Even though I am sure I am putting myself in harm's way from the prison administration and probably the Bureau of Prisons itself, I can no longer stand by and let this man lay here night after night in agony and perhaps die helplessly with our cell door locked and no way to get him emergency treatment. You can tell the reporter my name and that I am in Austin unit in cell 1774 at FCI Bastrop."

Dave Burgess who, as even Tim Elam had noticed, was often his own worst enemy.

*****

To: Mr Patrick George
Austin Statesman Newspaper
Austin, Texas
April 4, 2011
Dear Mr. George,

This is David Burgess at FCI Bastrop. As I am sure you are aware, I am the former cellie of the inmate with terminal colon cancer here at FCI Bastrop. Because of the somewhat esoteric security issues, I do not believe I am allowed to mention his name at this time. I believe you already have copies of my 4 previous news-letters concerning the on-going health & safety issues we are facing here in the Austin unit at FCI Bastrop. If you do not have copies, I am sure my friend Glen will forward them to you. If you need his telephone number and or e-mail address let me know and I will e-mail them to you.

Now to update you on what is going on now concerning the sick inmate. I know that he called you this morning (Monday 4/4/11) and gave you his name. But because of the intense medication he is taking I am not sure he is communicating his thoughts very well.

One of the main on-going problems he is now facing, is the fact that he is on so many heavy pain meds that he is almost helpless when it comes to normal everyday living issues. His current meds for pain are: In the morning he is given two 5/325mg tablets of OxyCODONE/Acetaminophen (Percocet.) At noon he is given two more Percocets and two 30mg capsule of MORPHINE SULFATE. In the evening he is given two more Percocets and another dose of MORPHINE SULFATE. As you can imagine, he is pretty much out of it when it comes to any sort of self-help.

For some unknown reason, the medical administration staff here at F.C.I Bastrop seems to take the stand that the sick inmate can care for himself. On one occasion the staff nurse was called to the unit to clean up one of his many blood spills. When she got here, she read us the riot act and told us to never bother her again to clean up his mess. She also said that we were not to clean it up, and that we were to tell him to get down on his hands and knees and clean up his own mess. This happened a week ago while he was receiving treatments from the "South Austin Cancer Treatment Center Radiation Oncology Team."

Now the Radiation Treatment has been completed and he has now started a regiment of Chemotherapy drugs.

The three Chemotherapy drugs are: One Capecitabine (Xeloda) pill once a day plus two intravenous I.V. drugs I believe once a week. They are; Bevacizumab(Avastin) and Oxaliplatin (Eloxatin.) The warnings on the information sheets

176

that he brought from the cancer treatment center regarding the new medications are distressful to say the least.

The sheets start out by saying stating, IMPORTANT THINGS TO REMEMBER: Most people do not experience all of the side-effects listed. Some but not all side-effects besides the normal side effects of Weakness, Hair loss, and Pain, are: Nausea, Vomiting, Upper respiratory infection, Low white & red blood count,(increased risk of infection) Kidney problems, Nose bleed, Diarrhea, Mouth sores, Dizziness, High to severe high blood pressure, Wound healing complications, Hemorrhage, Difficulty swallowing, Shortness of breath, Jaw spasms, Abnormal tongue, Hand Foot syndrome, and Blood clots that might lead to stroke/potentially life threatening conditions.

There is also a section heading called: SELF HELP TIPS. Under this section it explains what the drugs do to your immune system and how you can prevent further dangerous complications. It says regarding the chemo drugs: Cancerous tumors are characterized by cell division, which is no longer controlled as it is in normal tissue. Normal cells stop dividing when they come into contact with like cells, (known as contact inhibition.) Cancerous cells lose the ability...

The ability of Chemotherapy to kill cancer cells depends on its ability to halt cell division. Usually, the drugs work by damaging the RNA or DNA that tells the cell how to copy itself in division. If the cells are unable to divide, they die. The Chemo drugs also induce Apoptosis.

Chemotherapy is most effective at killing cells that are rapidly dividing. UNFORTUNATELY, Chemotherapy does NOT know the difference between the cancerous cells and the normal cells. The Normal cells will grow back and be healthy, but in the meantime, side effects do occur.

One of the main self-help tips mentioned is: YOU MAY BE AT RISK OF INFECTION SO TRY TO AVOID LARGE CROWDS OR PEOPLE WITH COLDS. The unit where the sick inmate lives, houses at this time, more than 300 inmates. And I must say, I have never seen so many inconsiderate folks coughing in your face, or into the telephone handset, and spitting on the ground right in front of you.

This can not possibly be a safe environment for any person on Chemotherapy. This sick inmate needs to be moved to a proper medical unit where he can be assisted by trained personnel. Not by two inmates who have absolutely no medical training.

One more important issue that comes to mind is the issue of monitoring for infection. The fact sheet states if a person on Chemotherapy has temperature of over 100.5 f, contact the health care provider immediately. We brought this issue up with the health care folks here at FCI Bastrop and told them we had nothing to monitor his temperature with. They told us not to worry about it and that he is at no risk of infection because of all the drugs he is taking. They also told us if he starts to feel warm to the touch, we can treat him with a damp towel on his forehead.

While I was at the medical clinic here today, I noticed a certificate on the wall issued by the "Joint Commission on Health Care Accreditation." It states that FCI Bastrop is an "Ambulatory Health Care Accreditation Facility" #72232 awarded on July 10, 2010 for the period of 39 months. And it states if there are any questions, to contact them at www.jointcommission.org

Maybe someone out there in the world could contact them and find out just what that certificate represents. And then just for grins, let me and everyone else here at FCI Bastrop know.

I am still as close as e-mail if you have any questions. At least at the time of this writing I still have e-mail access. With Respect, David Burgess 41278-048

*****

The Warden called Burgess into his office and told him bluntly, "Don't do that again." Burgess lost his job at the hobby shop and went back to work for the landscaping department. He was paid $5.95 after the first month. Two months later he became the "landscaping clerk, doing the payroll sheets for about 100 inmates." He also began repairing landscaping tools and eventually his pay soared to $36 in one month.

As his appeals became more and more hopeless Burgess also began to turn to God. ``For whom the Lord loveth he chasteneth, and scourgeth every son whom he receiveth."

"And, let me leave you with this thought," Burgess wrote.

"The day when He stood alone
And felt the hearts of man like stone,
And knew He came but to atone-
that day 'He held His peace.'
"They witnessed falsely to His word,
They bound Him with a cruel cord,
And mocking proclaimed Him Lord;
'But He held His peace.'
"They spat upon Him in the face,
They dragged Him from place to place,
They heaped upon Him all disgrace;
'But He held His peace.'
"My friend, have you for far much less,
With rage, which you call righteousness,
Resented slights with great distress?
'Your Savior held His peace.'

"After reading that, I feel in my heart, by comparison, my problems are so insignificant."

In an issue of *Dave's World Behind The Barbed Wire* Burgess wrote, "Anyway, the object of the class is for each student (there are eight of us) to pick a book of our individual choice and during the class each of us talks about the books we are reading. It is very casual. I am reading C.S. Lewis' *Mere Christianity*."

Burgess closed another newsletter with, "At this time in my life, where I have been ripped away from my family and friends, I know that the only two I can truly count on for my daily safety is the Lord and myself. In that order. GOD bless you All. Love and Respect, Dave, alone in the lone star state."

In 2012 he wrote, "I am here in prison doing 15 years for a crime I did not commit. And it is not just any crime. Sex offenders in prison are bad juju. Not many convicted sex offenders walk federal prison yards without getting smashed on. Sex offenders wear their crime on their sleeve and you can spot them from across the yard. I did not do the crime so I do not act the part. Everyone here knows what I was convicted of and few believe any of it. Everyone gives me a wide space, not because I am covered with club tattoos. I have no tattoos. But I am sure it is because of my club affiliation. Other inmates are not afraid of me, but I am sure they are aware of what I represent."

"I will continue to walk with my head held high. I will do nothing to start an altercation, but it has already been proven that I will not run away from one either. I have come to look at this time in prison as just another part of the wild life I continue to live."

*****

Burgess' final appeal was to Judge Johnson to reconsider his rulings in the case. What Burgess' attorneys in this appeal were really after was a chance to have the evidence against Burgess, the lewd photographs and writings that Anderson kept displaying to jurors and witnesses, examined by a computer forensics expert.

The main argument in the long appeal was that Burgess had been denied an effective counsel. And there were numerous instances alleged in the appeal where Jim Barrett's performance as a defender was questionable.

At least partly because Judge Johnson gave prosecutor James Anderson multiple lengthy continuances to respond to the appeal, almost three years elapsed between the filing of the appeal and a hearing on the matter in Judge Johnson's court.

There were reasons to stall. In general, federal courts are required to preserve evidence after convictions. The evidence used to convict Burgess would have been stored at the Cheyenne offices of the Internet Crimes Against Children Task Force. There is a strong possibility that the people preserving the evidence are the same people who framed Dave Burgess. So there is a strong possibility that the evidence used to convict Burgess has been destroyed. If Judge Johnson could be persuaded to convene an evidentiary hearing, and the evidence in the Burgess case could not be produced, Dave Burgess would be set free.

The appeal cited 16 instances in which Barrett had acted unprofessionally or incompetently and seven instances where Johnson himself had erred and deprived Burgess of his right to a fair trial. In a 149 pages decision filed on May 23rd, 2013 Johnson denied all 23 claims for relief and concluded, "For all the reasons stated, petitioner Burgess's motion is denied. The file, records, and all submissions by the parties conclusively show he is not entitled to the relief he seeks. Accordingly, no evidentiary hearing is required."

Made in the USA
Middletown, DE
28 August 2015